CASE

UNSOLVED

FILES

**CASE No. 002** THE ROCK

This book is dedicated to the men & women who have worked this case.

Photographs pages 100–103 used courtesy of the FBI.

Balzer + Bray is an imprint of HarperCollins Publishers.
HarperAlley is an imprint of HarperCollins Publishers.

Unsolved Case Files: Jailbreak at Alcatraz:
Frank Morris & the Anglin Brothers' Great Escape
Copyright © 2021 by Thomas G. Sullivan

ISBN 978-0-06-299155-3 — ISBN 978-0-06-299154-6 (paperback)

The artist used pens, pencils, and Adobe Photoshop to create the illustrations for this book.
Typography by Tom Sullivan and Dana Fritts
21 22 23 24 25  GPS  10 9 8 7 6 5 4 3 2 1
❖
First Edition

UNSOLVED CASE FILES

# JAILBREAK AT ALCATRAZ

Frank Morris & the Anglin Brothers'
Great Escape

## by TOM SULLIVAN

BALZER + BRAY
Imprints of HarperCollinsPublishers

THIS IS A TRUE STORY.

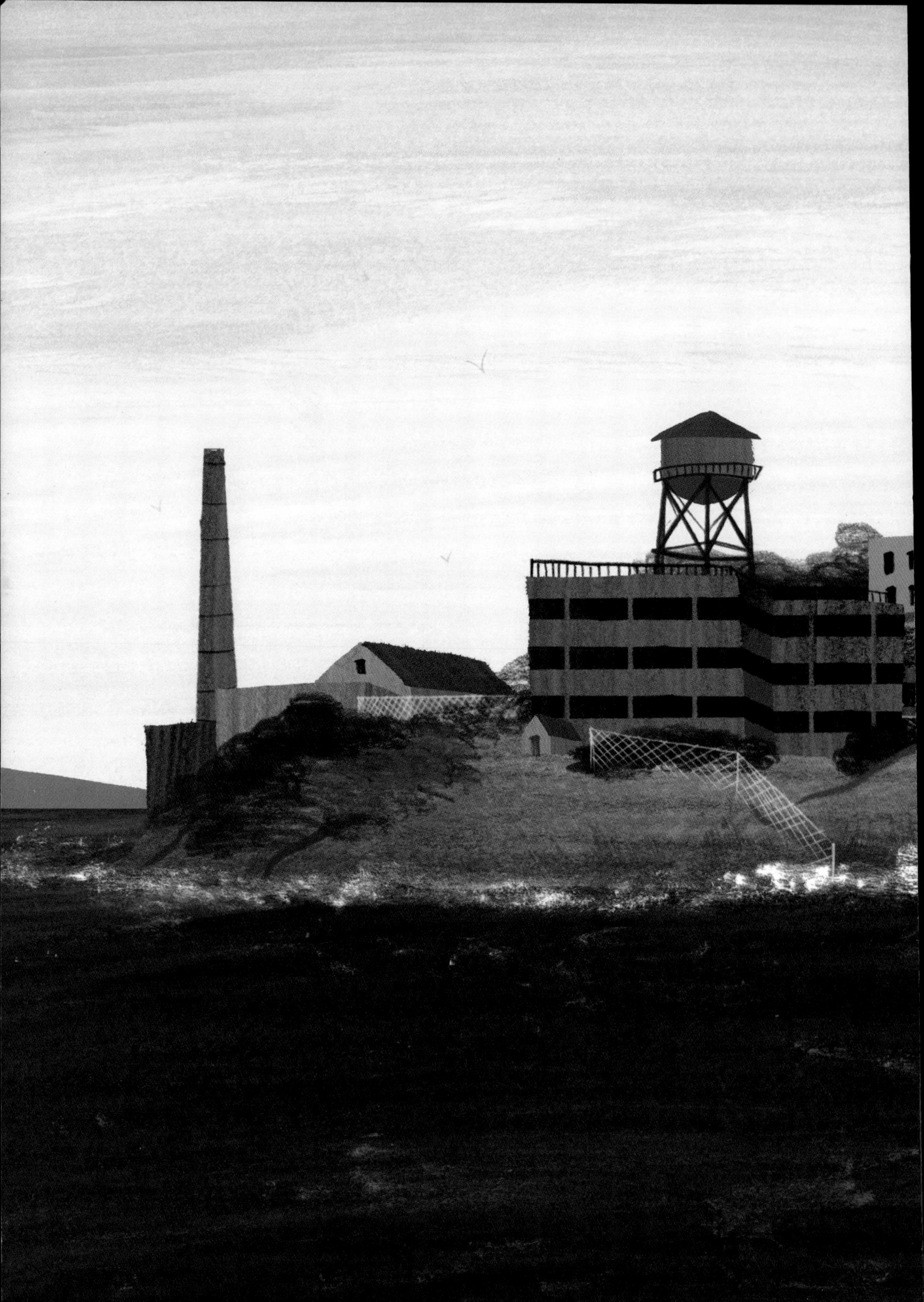

# PART ONE:
# WAKE UP, DUMMY

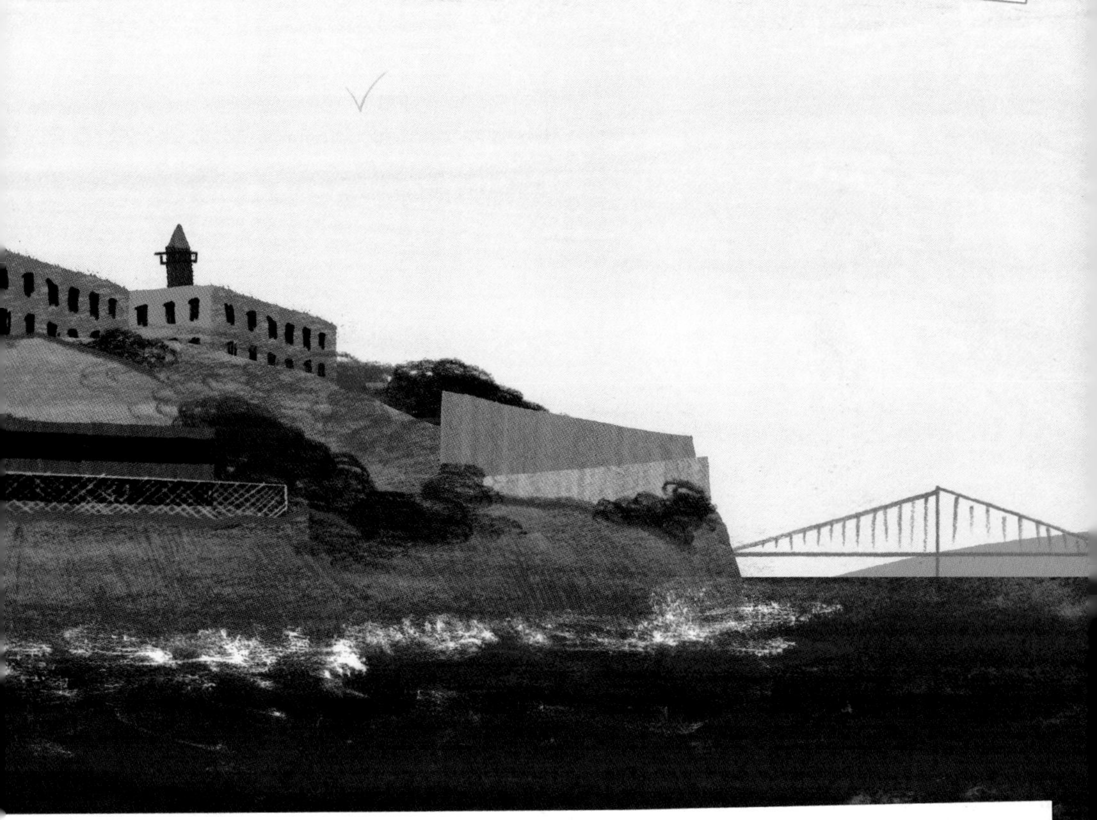

**JUNE 12, 1962**

**SAN FRANCISCO BAY, CALIFORNIA**

**7:00 a.m.**

The morning bell rang out at the ALCATRAZ FEDERAL PENITENTIARY, and the criminals incarcerated there began their day.

Designed by the first warden, JAMES A. JOHNSTON, the daily schedule on "The Rock" was very strict. At precisely 7:00 a.m., the prisoners woke up, got dressed, and made their beds.

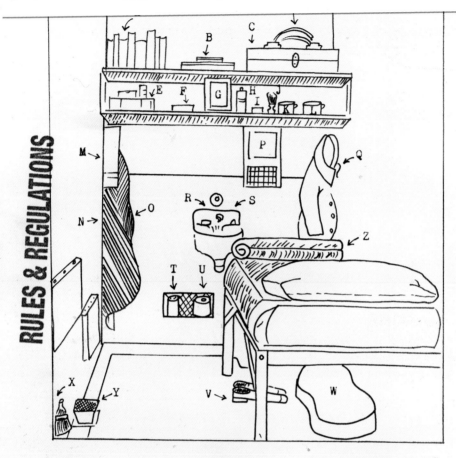

# RULES & REGULATIONS

B
C
E
F
G
H
I
J
K
L
M
N
O
P
Q
R
S
T
U
V
W
X
Y
Z


A — 12 Books(Maximum)
B — Personal Papers
C — Paint Box etc.
D — Radio Headphones
E — Ash Tray & Tobacco
F — Extra Soap
G — Mirror
H — Toothpowder
I — Razor & Blades
j — Shaving Brush
K — Shaving Mug
L — Drinking Cup
M — Face Towell
N — Bathrobe
O — Raincoat
P — Calendar
Q — Coat & Cap
R — Soap
S — Sink Stopper
T — Cleaning Powder
U — Toilet Tissue
V — Extra SHoes & Slippers
W — Musical Instrument/Case
X — Broom
Y — Trash Basket
Z — Extra Blankets

N.B. Extra Blanket is to be folded neatly at foot of bed. Pillow at the head of the bed toward the bars. Blankets are to be tucked in under the mattress. Shoes, slippers and musical instrument & case are to be under the bed with the shoes or slippers under the leading edge of the bed.

Next, they had to arrange their personal items in the mandated order on their assigned shelves. The inmates were then required to clean the sink and toilet, wipe down their cell's bars, sweep the floor, and fold the seat and table up against the wall. Once they finished their morning chores, they awaited the second bell, which would ring after the guards had completed the count.

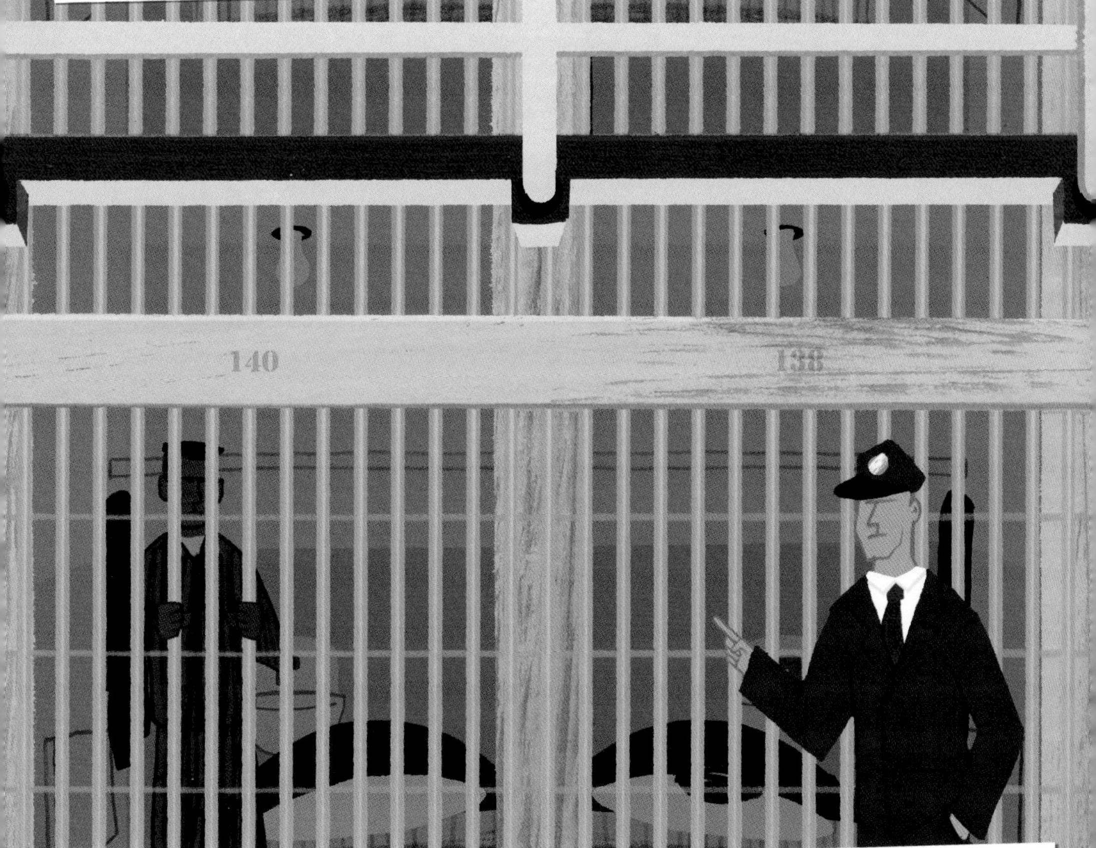
140
138

In the days before surveillance equipment, the prison guards physically counted the inmates a total of nineteen times every twenty-four hours so they could monitor their whereabouts. It was important to do so because of the nature of the prisoners. No one was ever sentenced to serve time on Alcatraz specifically; instead, the country's most heinous criminals were transferred to The Rock when they proved to be too much for other federal prisons to handle.

**7:18 a.m.**

Corrections officer LAWRENCE BARTLETT was performing the morning count and making his way down "Michigan Ave.," which was the nickname given to the main corridor between A and B blocks. But when BARTLETT reached cell 138, inmate number AZ-1441, a career criminal named FRANK MORRIS, was apparently still fast asleep.

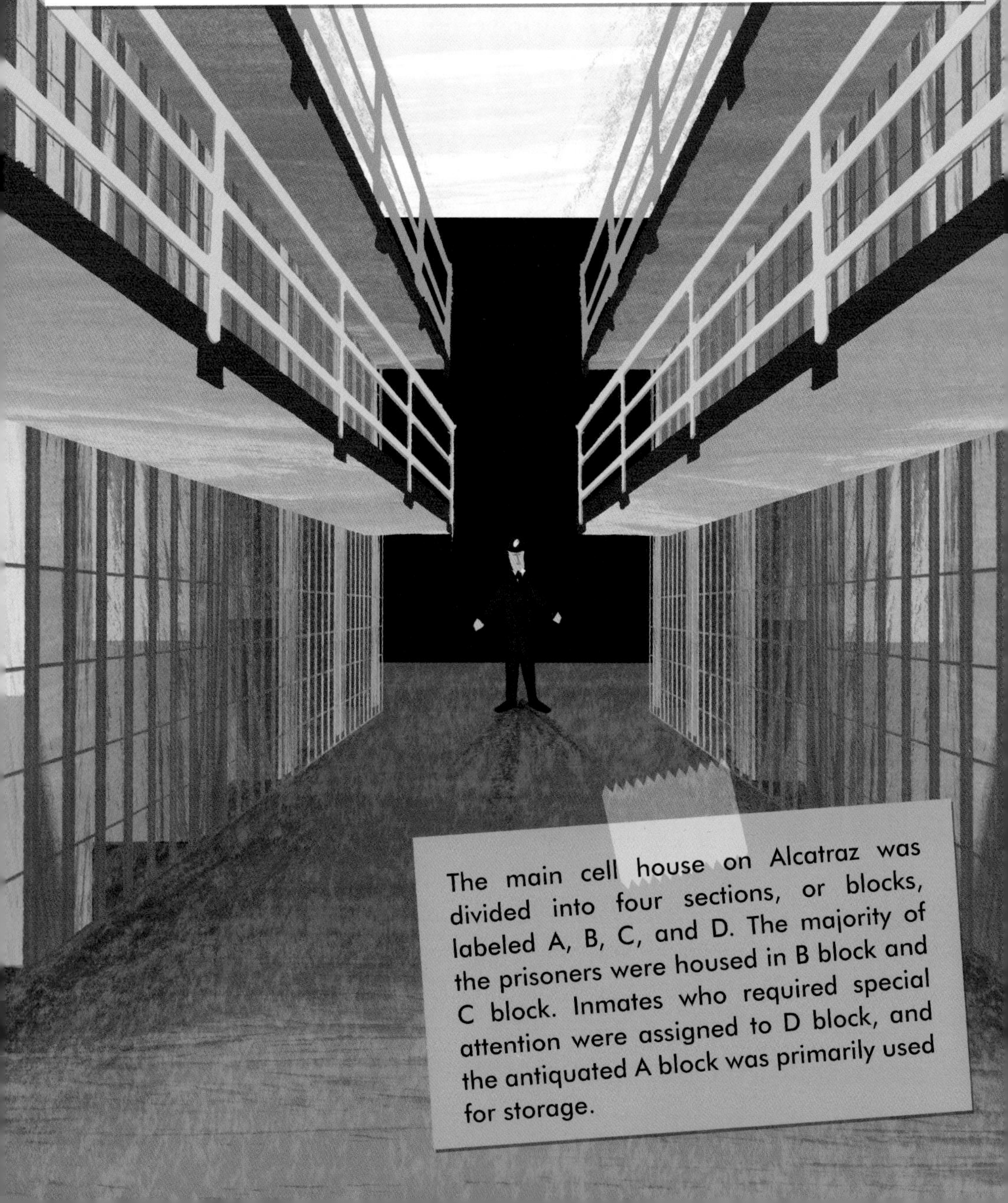

The main cell house on Alcatraz was divided into four sections, or blocks, labeled A, B, C, and D. The majority of the prisoners were housed in B block and C block. Inmates who required special attention were assigned to D block, and the antiquated A block was primarily used for storage.

Officer BARTLETT rapped his knuckles against the cell bars and instructed MORRIS to get up, or else there would be consequences.

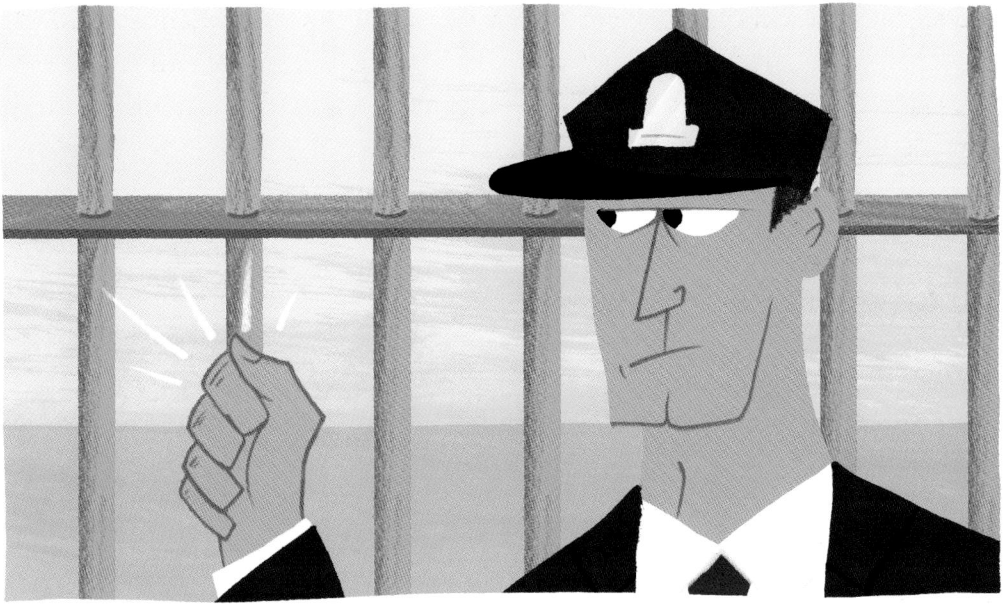

But there was no response.

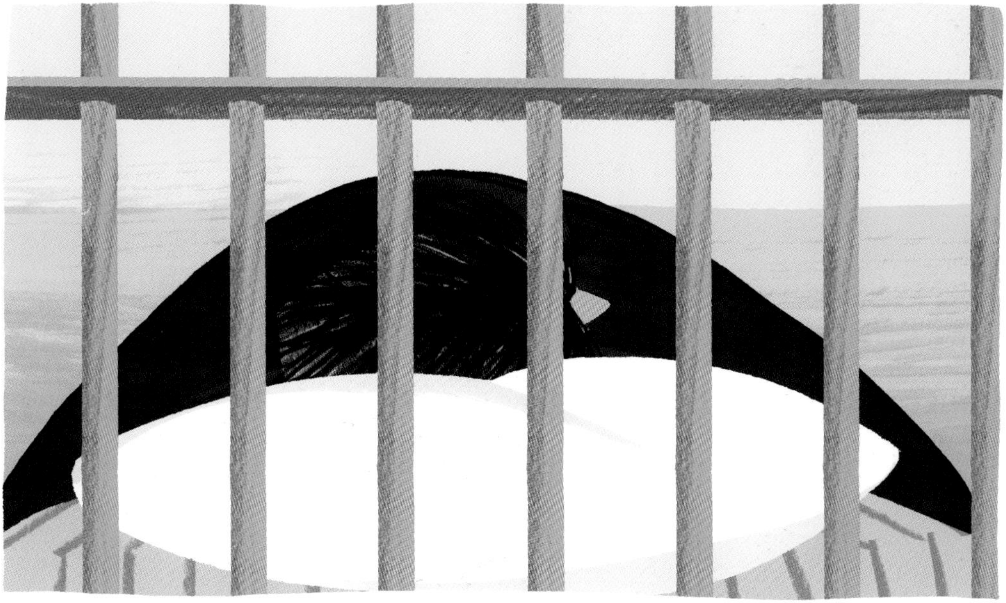

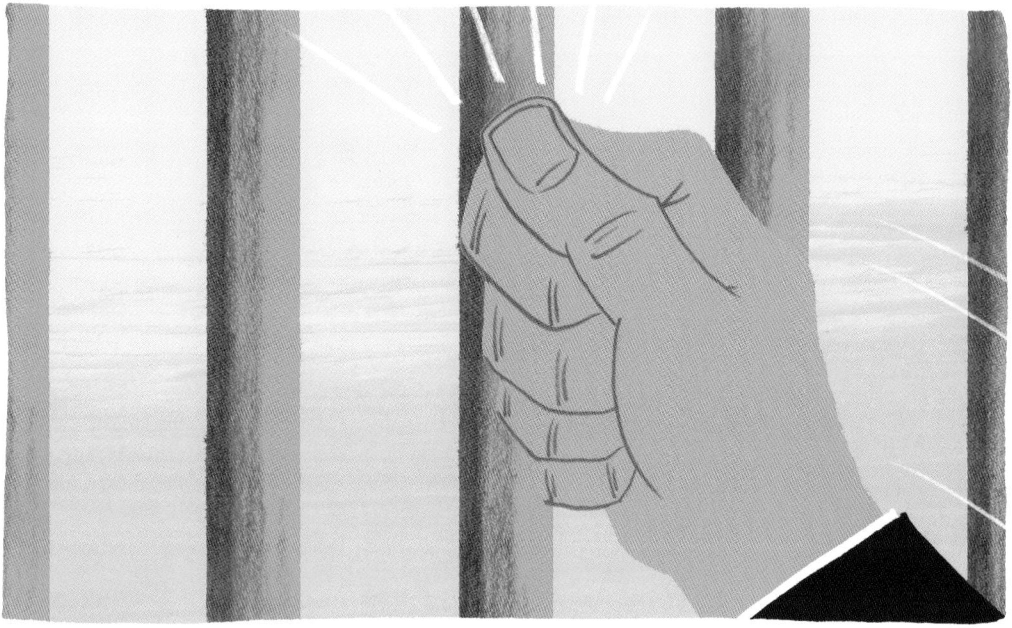

Once more, BARTLETT knocked on the bars in an attempt to wake the inmate. Finally, he reached in through the bars and gave MORRIS'S head a good shake.

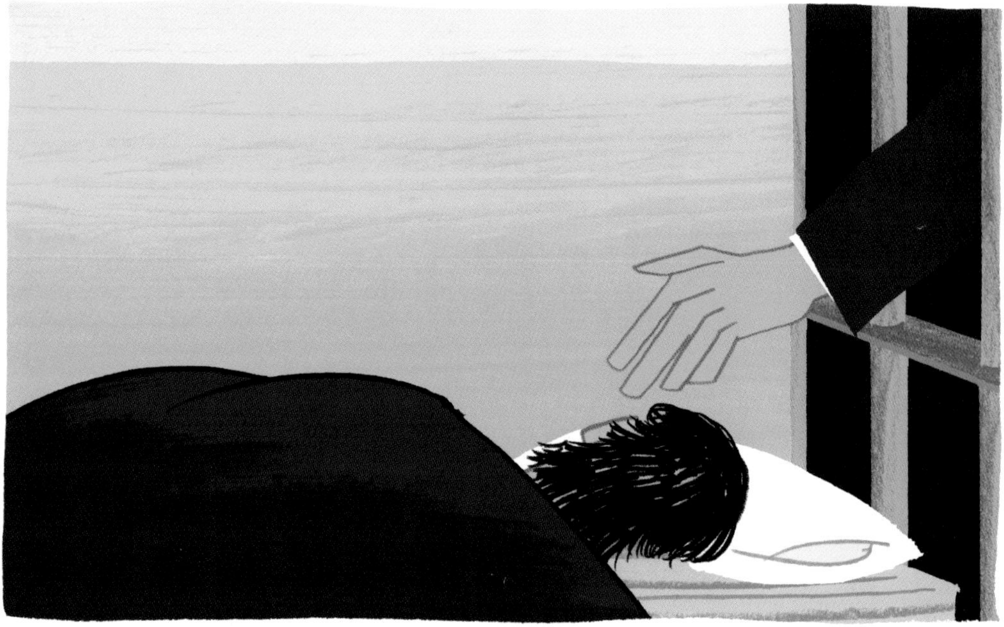

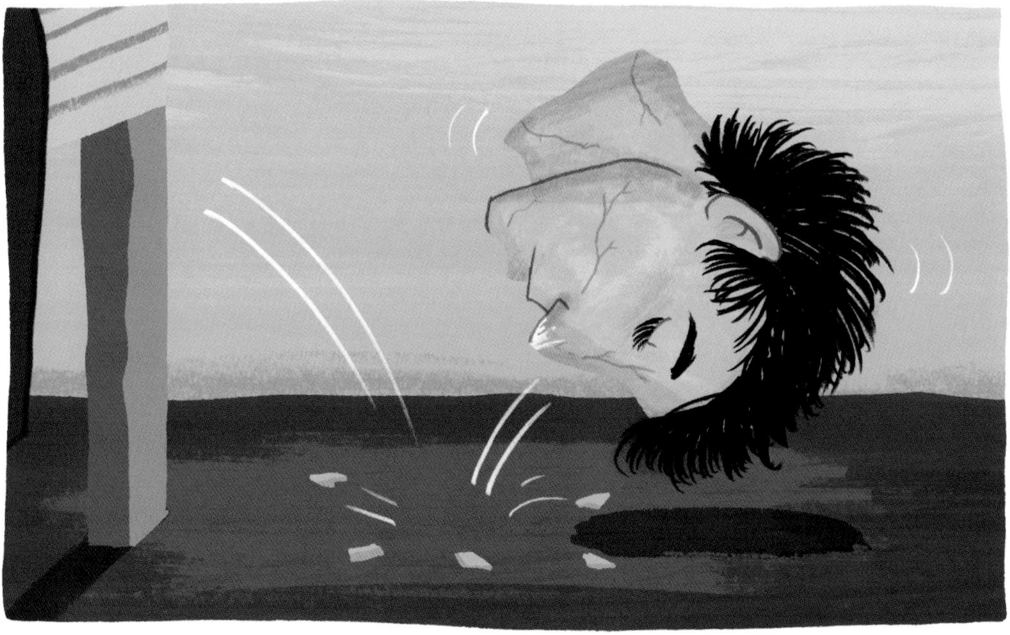

But to his shock, the head rolled off the pillow and smashed against the concrete floor!

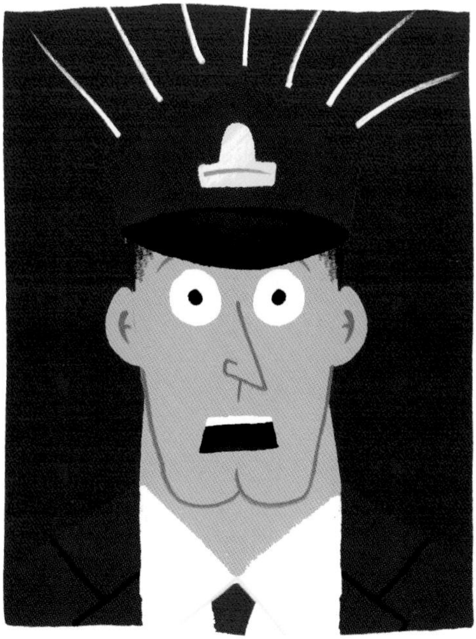

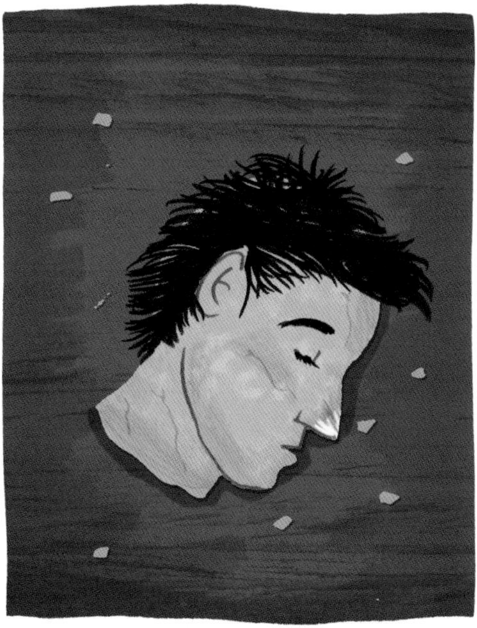

The other guards were quick to realize that in cells 150 and 152, brothers JOHN (AZ-1476) and CLARENCE (AZ-1485) ANGLIN had also failed to awaken.

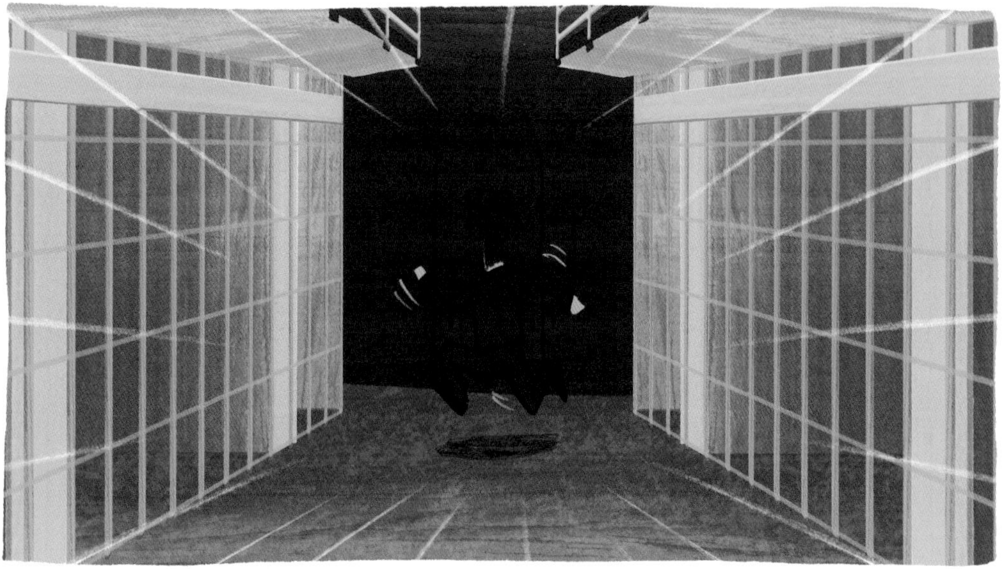

Inside those cells the corrections officers discovered the same thing found in MORRIS'S bed: blankets rolled up under the covers, meticulously crafted to look like a sleeping body, and crudely made (yet ingenious) papier-mâché heads, complete with real human hair.

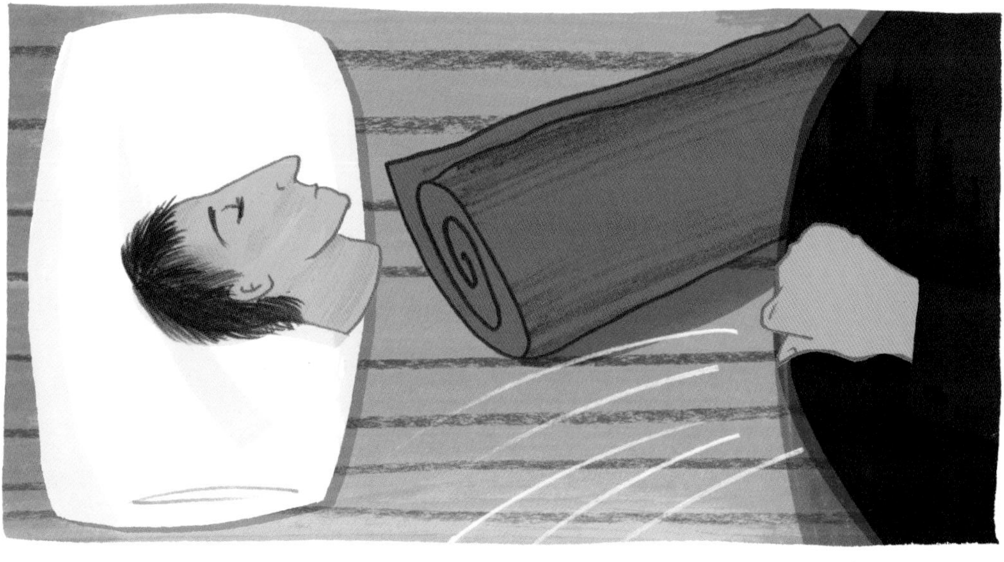

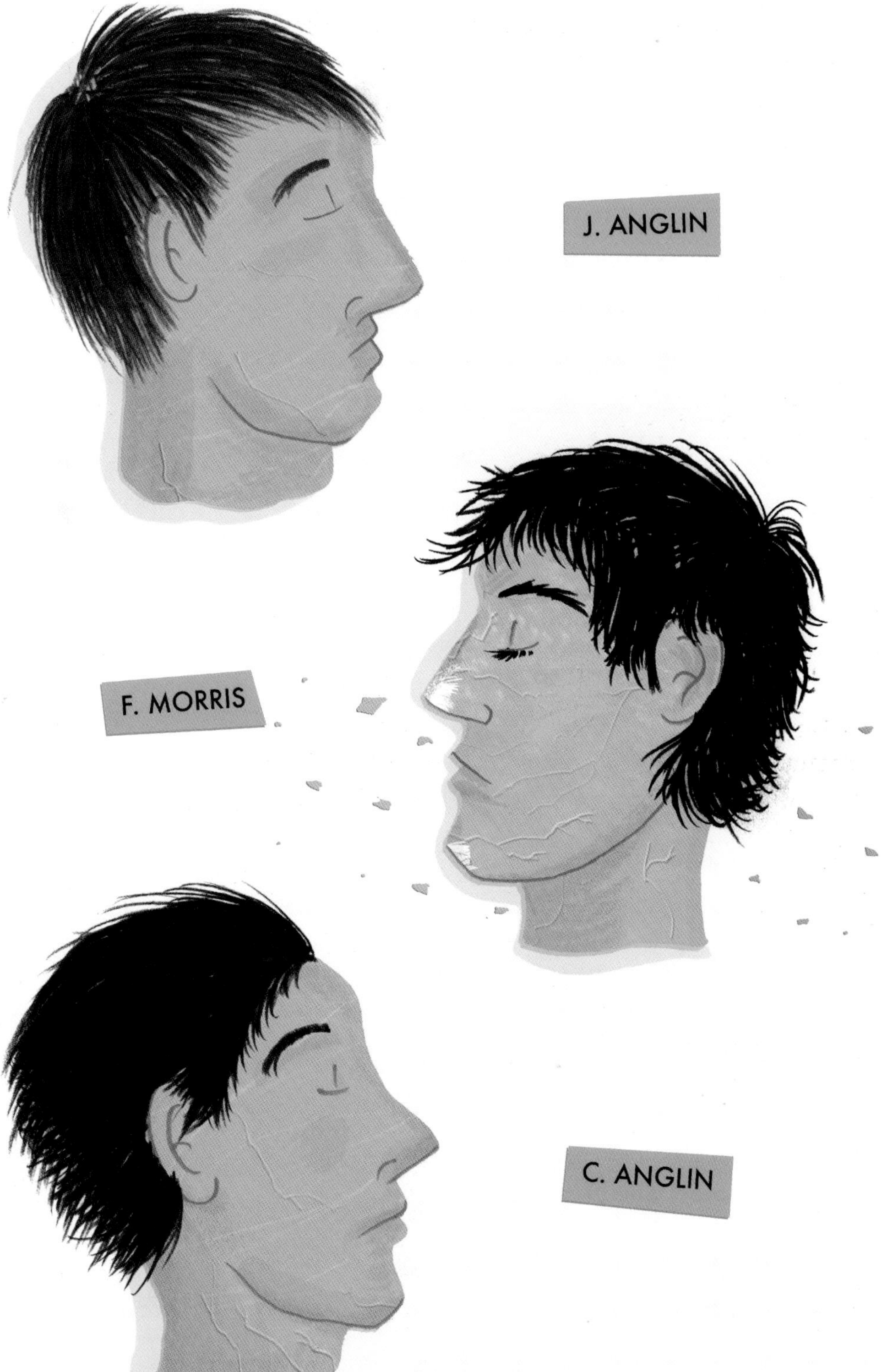
J. ANGLIN
F. MORRIS
C. ANGLIN

Meanwhile, in the residential area on the southeast side of the island, associate warden ARTHUR M. DOLLISON was reading the paper and eating breakfast when the telephone rang. The warden of Alcatraz, OLIN G. BLACKWELL, was away on vacation, but it was still unusual to be disturbed that early in the morning, and DOLLISON knew instantly that the phone call would not be good news.

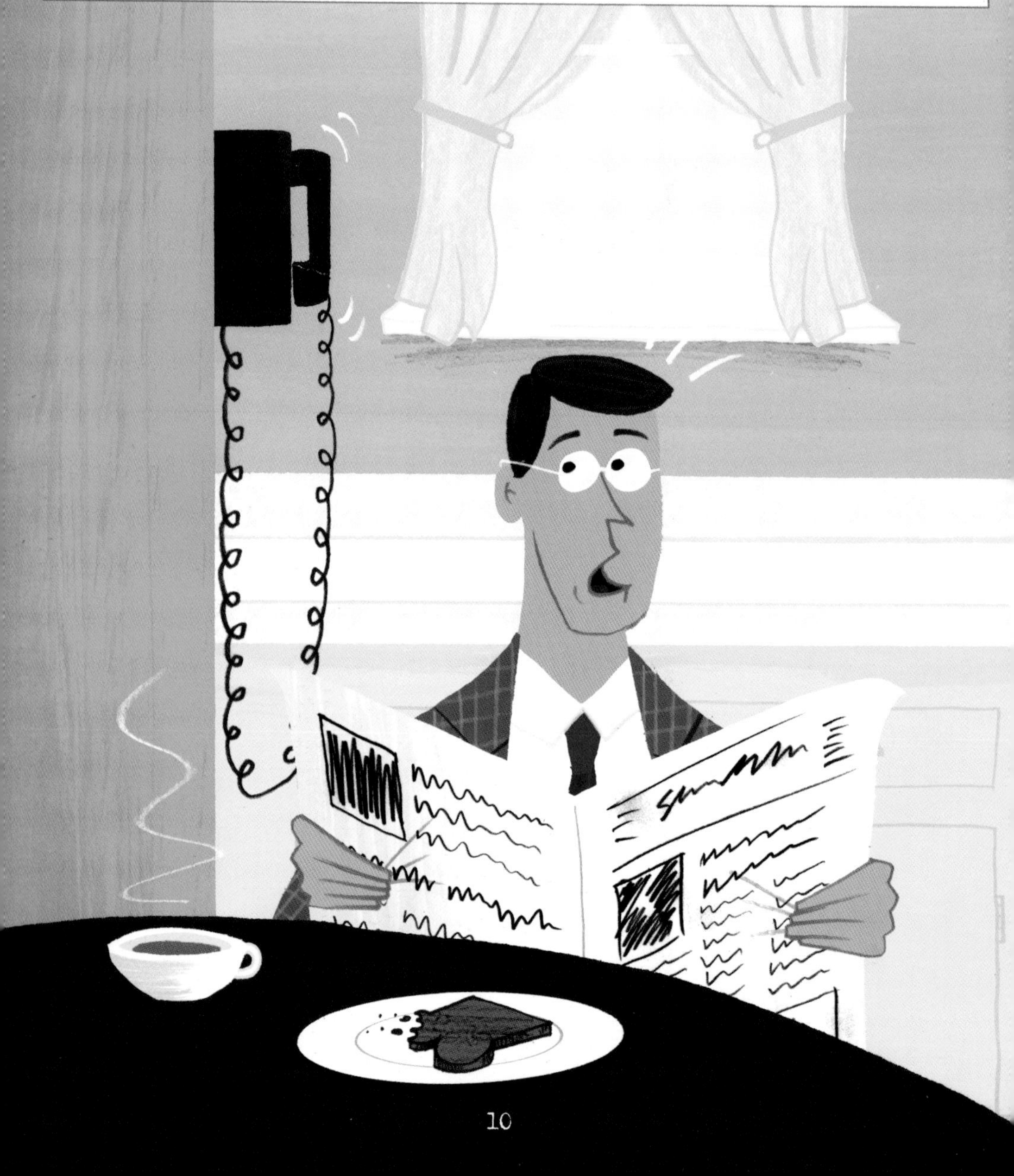

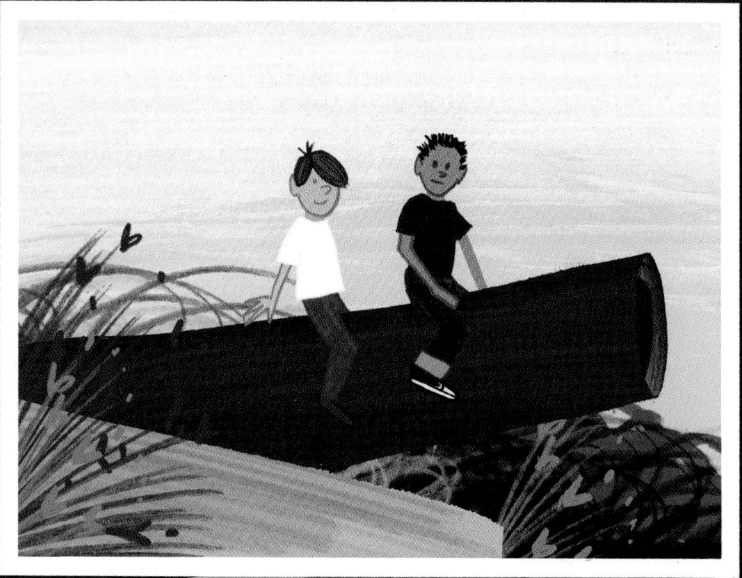

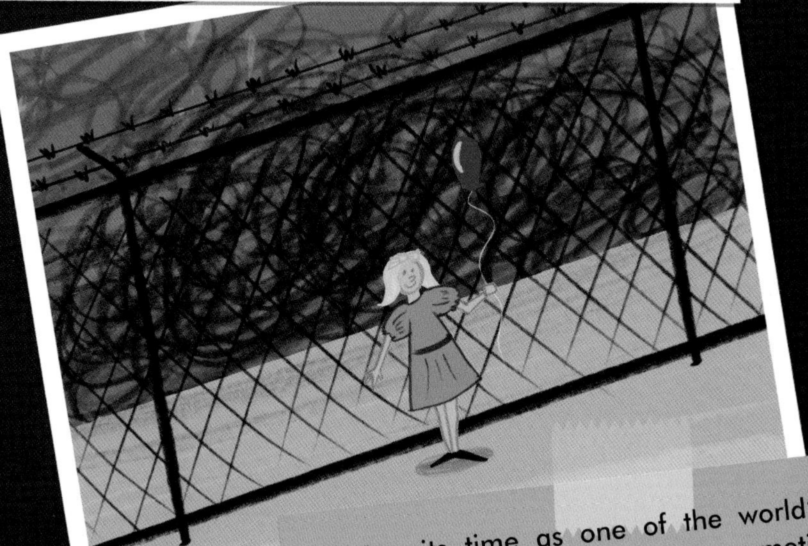

During its time as one of the world's most dangerous prisons, there were sometimes as many as fifty different families living on Alcatraz Island, and that included children. While some of the guards commuted to the island, many lived in the four-acre residential area, which included apartment buildings, cottages, and the warden's mansion. There was also a general store, a pool hall, a bowling alley, a Sunday school, and even a dance hall where the residents hosted parties.

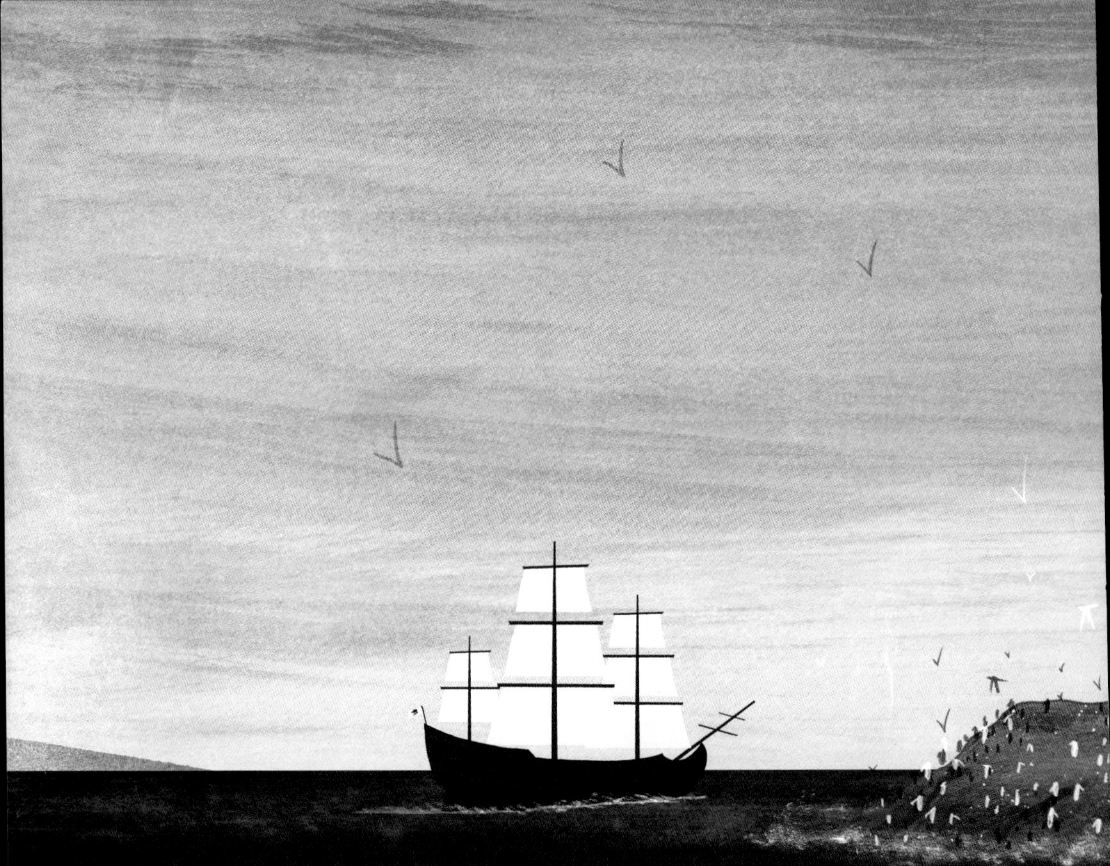

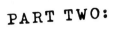

PART TWO:

# THE ISLAND OF THE PELICANS

Even though European explorers first sailed up the California coast in the late 1500s, it wasn't until the Spanish explorer JUAN MANUEL DE AYALA navigated the first ship through the GOLDEN GATE STRAIT in 1775 that the uninviting hunk of rock was given its first name. He dubbed the island La Isla de los Alcatraces, which translates literally to "The Island of the Pelicans."

La Isla de los Alcatraces went largely ignored except by the swarms of seabirds that roosted and defecated all over its jagged shore, earning it the nicknames Bird Island and White Island. The Spanish name was eventually shortened to Alcatraces, and then simply Alcatraz.

Alcatraz changed ownership from Spanish to Mexican hands, and was eventually sold for $5,000 to the military governor of California, GENERAL JOHN C. FRÉMONT. But the United States government seized the island under eminent domain, and by 1859, construction of Fort Alcatraz, and the first-ever lighthouse built on the West Coast, was completed.

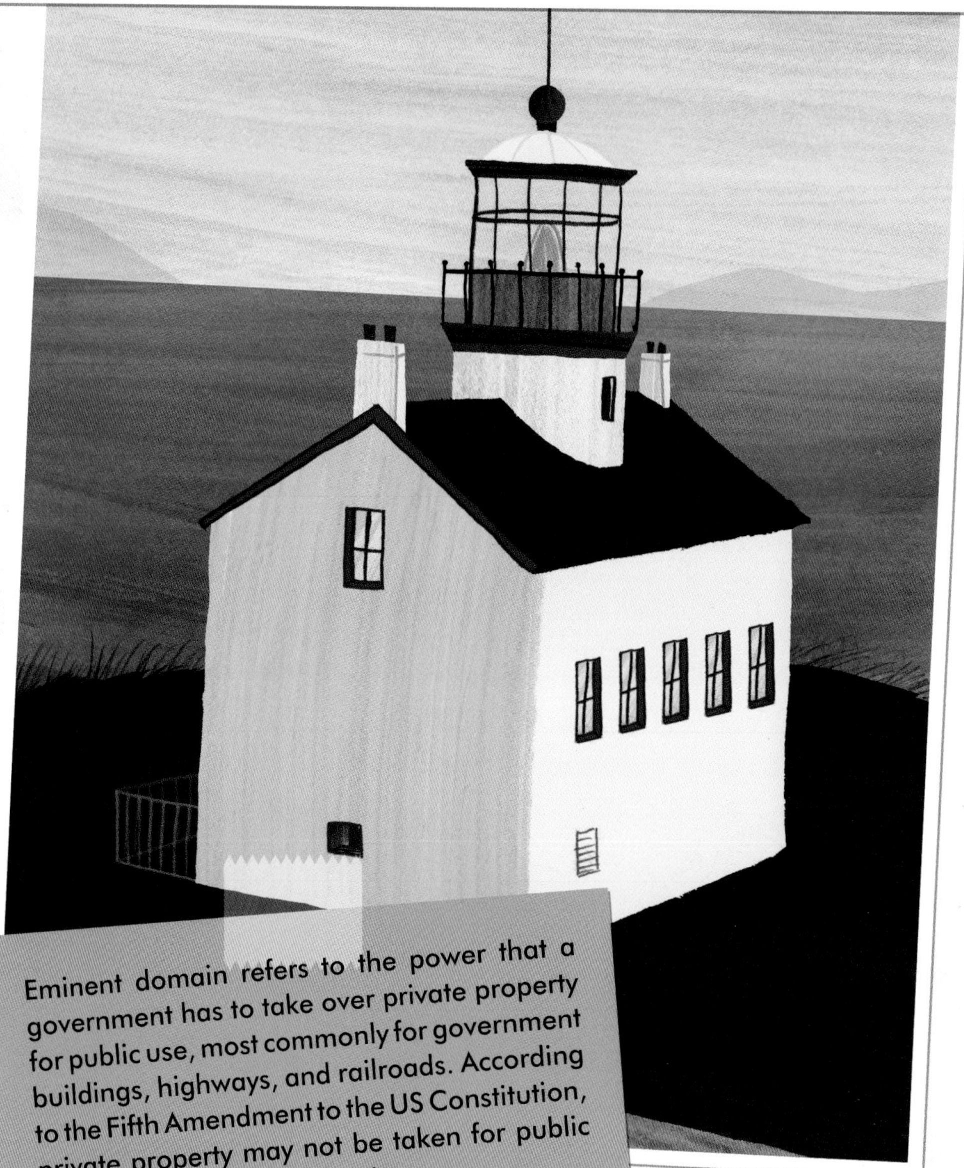

Eminent domain refers to the power that a government has to take over private property for public use, most commonly for government buildings, highways, and railroads. According to the Fifth Amendment to the US Constitution, private property may not be taken for public use without just compensation.

Its role as a fort was short-lived, however. In 1861, during the Civil War, it became a military prison, housing Confederate prisoners of war. Over the years, it continued to operate as a disciplinary barracks for the armed forces, and buildings were added to the island, including the main cell house in 1909. But a new era began for Alcatraz after Congress passed the Volstead Act in 1919, which ushered in Prohibition—and with it a deadly crime wave that rocked the country for more than a decade. The US government was in dire need of a better prison, and what better location than an isolated island surrounded by treacherous waters?

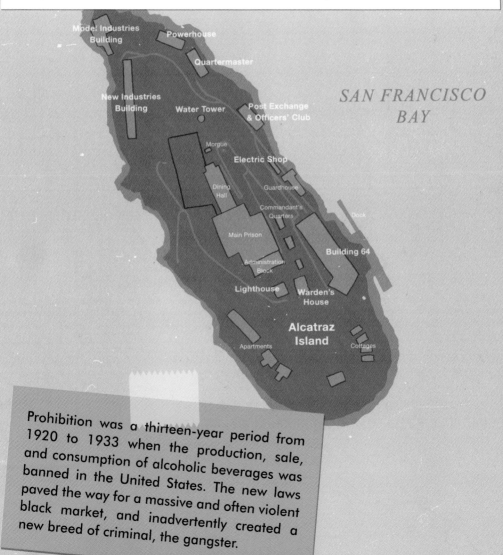

Model Industries Building

Powerhouse

Quartermaster

New Industries Building

Water Tower

Post Exchange & Officers' Club

SAN FRANCISCO BAY

Morgue

Electric Shop

Dining Hall

Guardhouse

Commandant's Quarters

Dock

Main Prison

Building 64

Administration Block

Lighthouse

Warden's House

Alcatraz Island

Apartments

Cottages

Prohibition was a thirteen-year period from 1920 to 1933 when the production, sale, and consumption of alcoholic beverages was banned in the United States. The new laws paved the way for a massive and often violent black market, and inadvertently created a new breed of criminal, the gangster.

JAMES A. JOHNSTON, the inaugural warden of Alcatraz, was hired in 1933 to transform the outdated facility into a maximum-security federal penitentiary.

JOHNSTON beefed up security in the B and C cell blocks by replacing the soft iron bars with hardened "tool-proof" steel. He installed automatic locks, erected barbed-wire fences, stationed every vantage point with armed guards, and even put bars on the sewers.

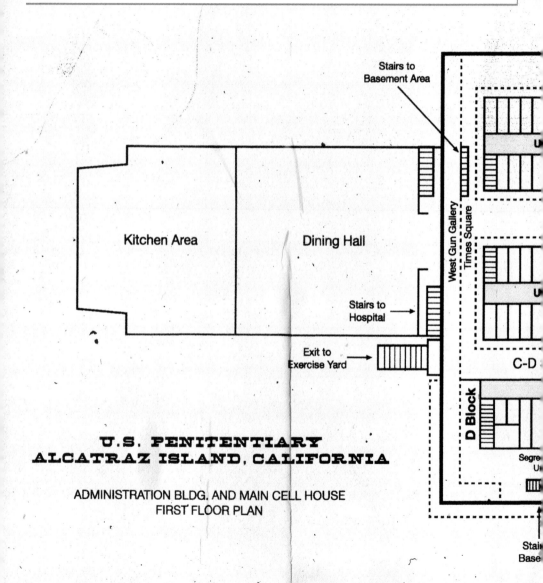

Stairs to
Basement Area

Kitchen Area

Dining Hall

West Gun Gallery

Times Square

Stairs to
Hospital

Exit to
Exercise Yard

C-D

D Block

Segre
U

U.S. PENITENTIARY
ALCATRAZ ISLAND, CALIFORNIA

ADMINISTRATION BLDG. AND MAIN CELL HOUSE
FIRST FLOOR PLAN

Stai
Base

The guards—or "bulls," as the convicts would call them—were hand-selected from other federal penitentiaries around the country, and trained both mentally and physically in military tactics.

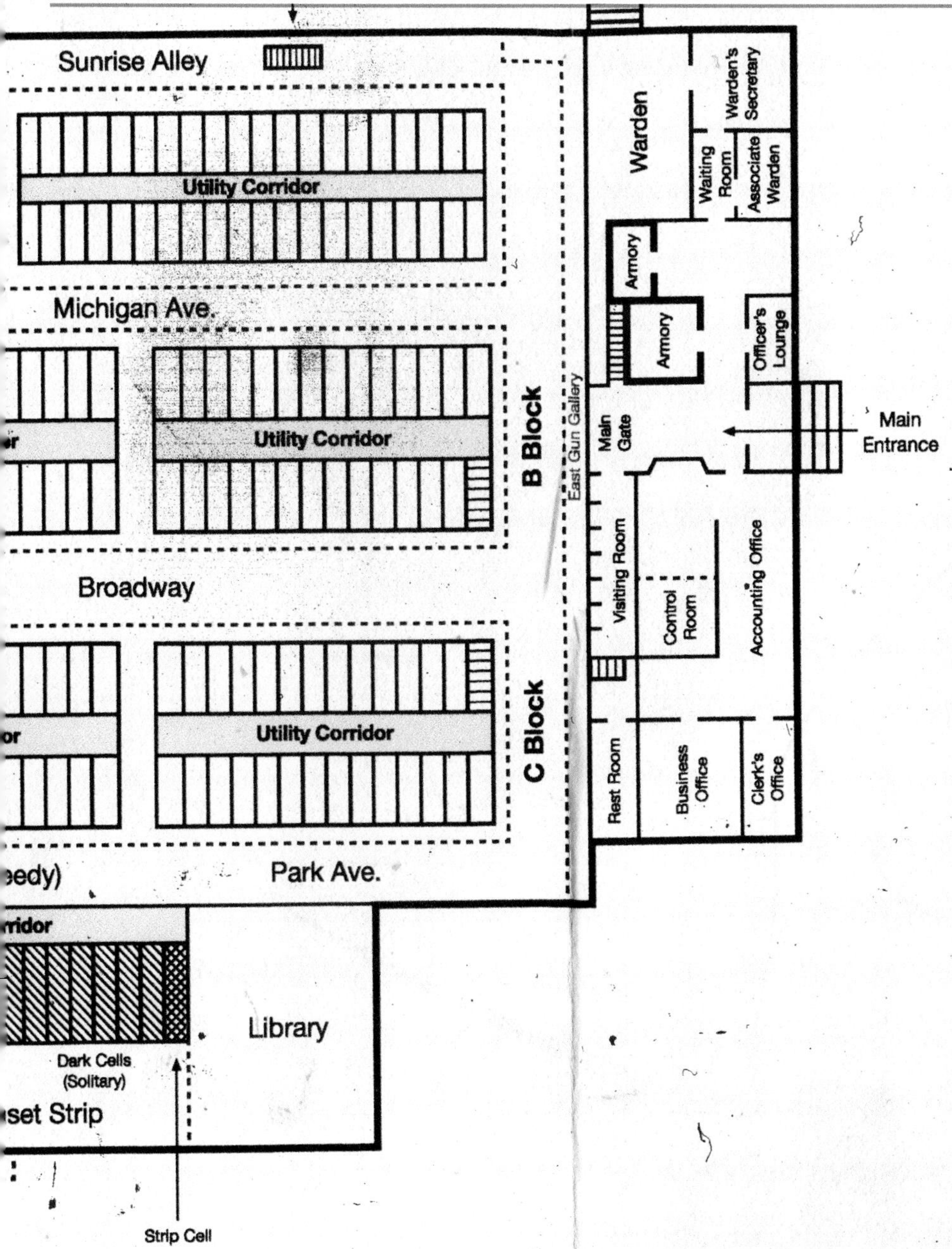
op
Sunrise Alley
Utility Corridor
Michigan Ave.
Utility Corridor
B Block
East Gun Gallery
Broadway
Utility Corridor
C Block
eedy)
Park Ave.
rridor
Library
Dark Cells
(Solitary)
set Strip
Strip Cell
Warden
Warden's Secretary
Waiting Room
Associate Warden
Armory
Armory
Officer's Lounge
Main Gate
Main Entrance
Visiting Room
Control Room
Accounting Office
Rest Room
Business Office
Clerk's Office

On August 11, 1934, the first batch of 137 prisoners arrived at the newly christened Alcatraz Federal Penitentiary, and less than two years later—on April 27, 1936—the first escape attempt was made.

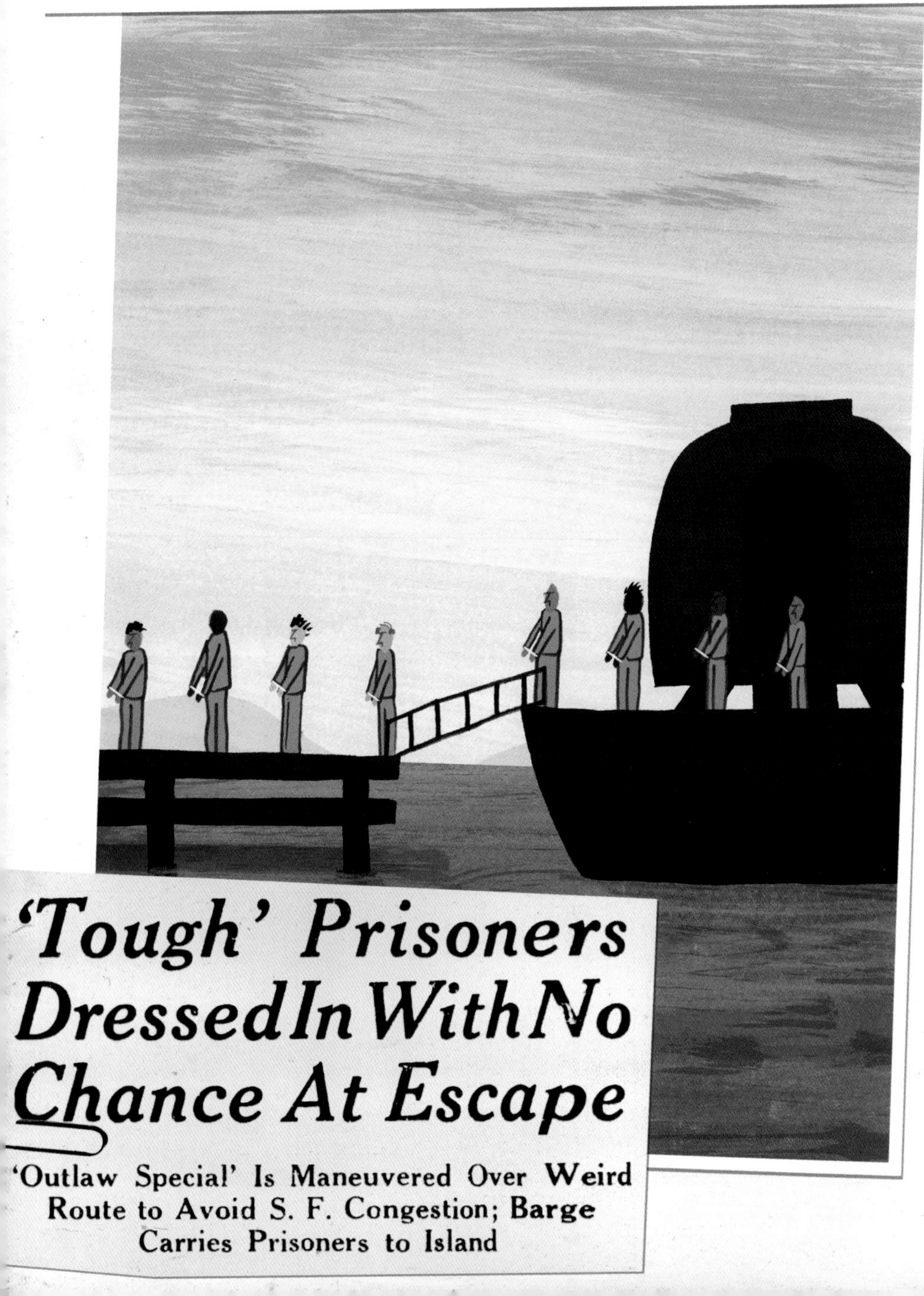

# 'Tough' Prisoners Dressed In With No Chance At Escape

**'Outlaw Special' Is Maneuvered Over Weird Route to Avoid S. F. Congestion; Barge Carries Prisoners to Island**

J. BOWERS

PART THREE:

# FLY THE COOP

The first attempt to escape from Alcatraz was made by JOSEPH BOWERS (AZ-210), a car thief and robber. BOWERS was burning trash on his work detail at the incinerator when he decided to make a run for it.

BOWERS scaled the perimeter fence. He ignored two warning shots and repeated verbal commands before the guard fired upon him. BOWERS was shot in the leg, and perished when he fell some fifty feet to the rocky shore below.

A work detail is a low-paying (or sometimes unpaid) job assigned to prisoners. On Alcatraz, inmates would start out with food service, maintenance, or general custodial work. As a reward for good behavior, they could be promoted to a job in the Industry Shop, where the prison serviced various military contracts, including laundry, tailoring, and cobbling, in addition to manufacturing items such as gloves, rubber mats, and brushes.

T. COLE

R. ROE

The second escape attempt was better planned than the first. On December 16, 1937, THEODORE COLE (AZ-258), a kidnapper and murderer, along with bank robber RALPH ROE (AZ-260), were working their details in the mat shop, recycling old car tires into rubber mats for the navy. After the work count following lunch, the guard on duty left the mat shop unattended while he patrolled the nearby blacksmith shop, and that's when COLE and ROE made their move. Using a hacksaw blade they had stolen, the inmates made the final cuts on the security bars they had spent the last few weeks chipping away at. After punching out a couple of panes of glass, then using a wrench to unbolt the gate in the chain-link fence, the convicts made their way down to the water's edge.

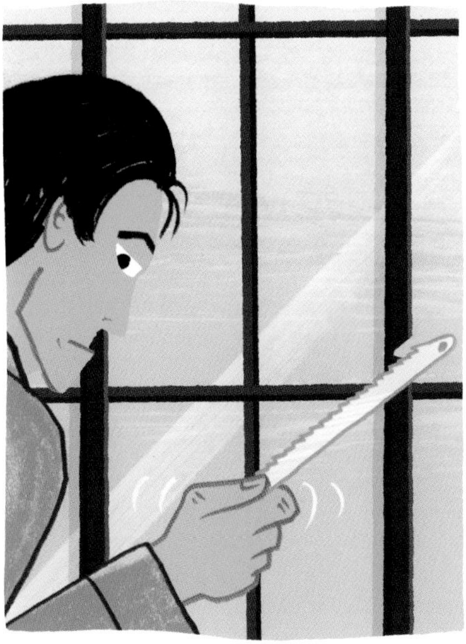

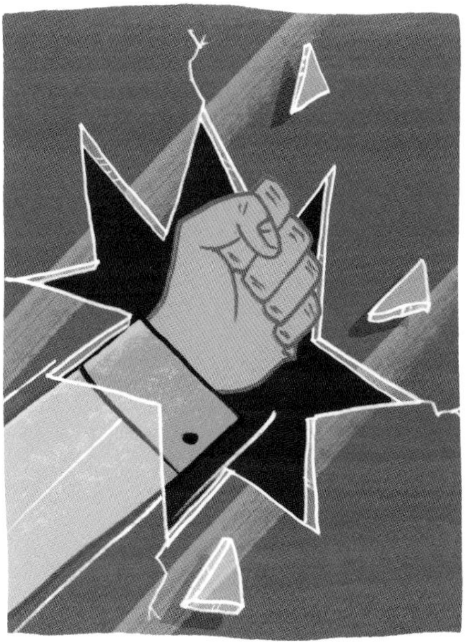

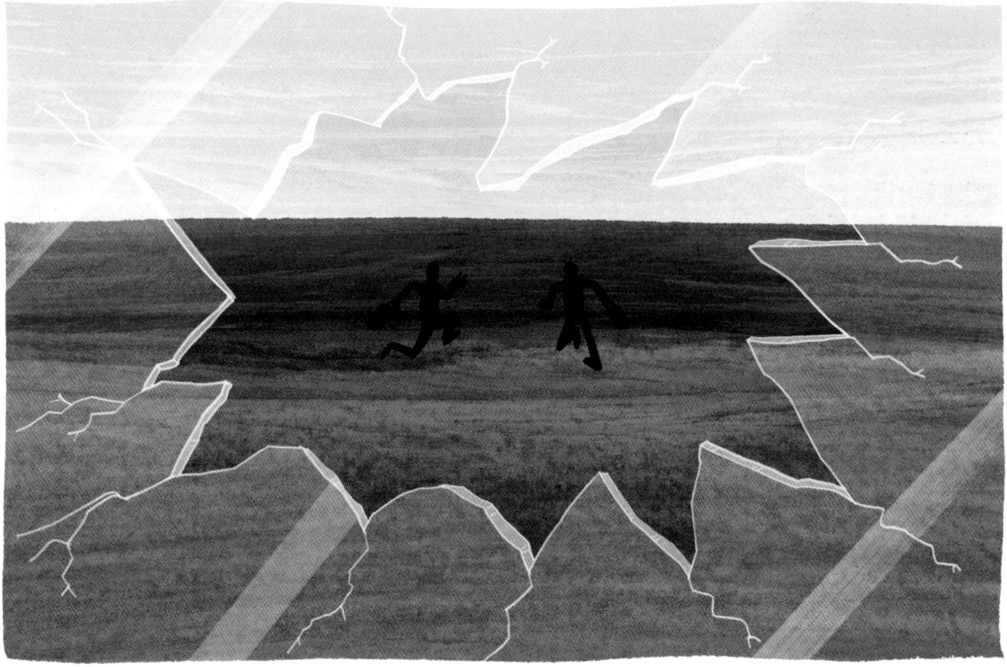

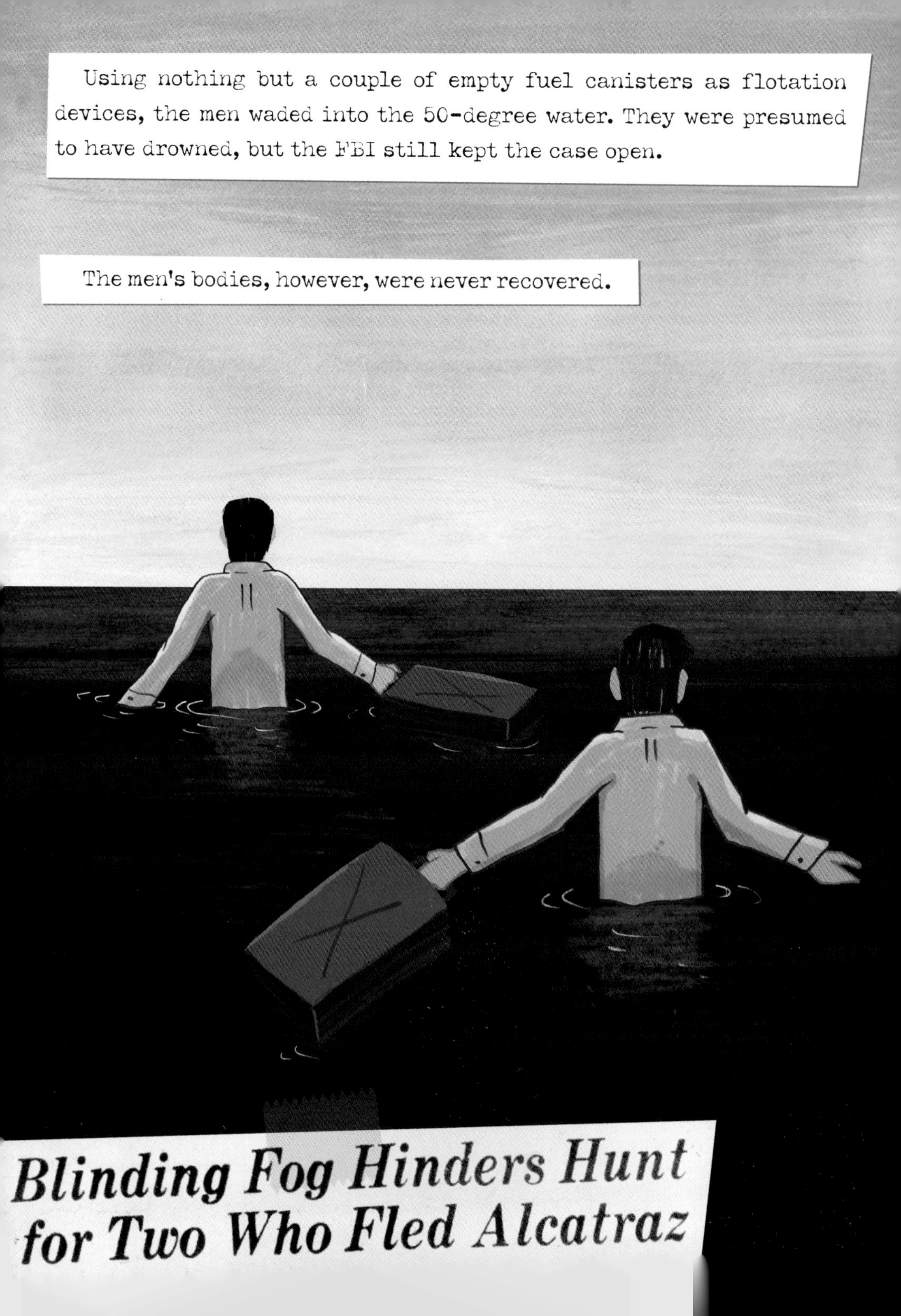
Using nothing but a couple of empty fuel canisters as flotation devices, the men waded into the 50-degree water. They were presumed to have drowned, but the FBI still kept the case open.
The men's bodies, however, were never recovered.
Blinding Fog Hinders Hunt for Two Who Fled Alcatraz

Over the next twenty-one years, there were ten additional escapes attempted by twenty-six different prisoners, and they all wound up either dead or recaptured.

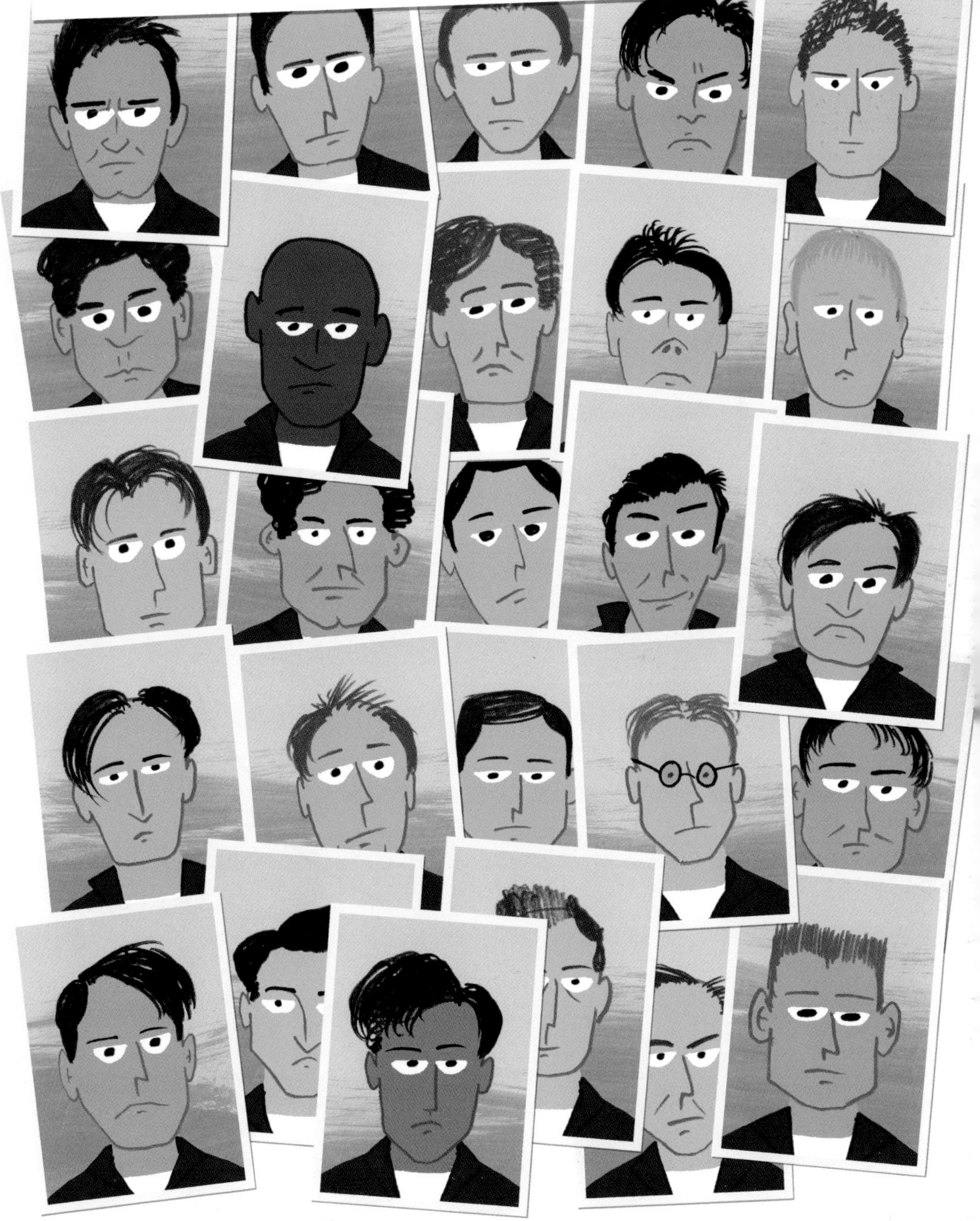

# Criminal History Report

| CONTRIBUTER OF FINGERPRINTS | NAME AND NUMBER | ARRESTED OR RECEIVED | CHARGE | DISPOSITION |
|---|---|---|---|---|
| PD, New Orleans, La. | FRANK LYONS #44506 | finger-printed 1/23/56 | held for Federal authorities in Parish prison | |
| USM, New Orleans, La. | FRANK LEE MORRIS #S223 | 9/13/56 | Attempt to escape while awaiting trial under an indictment | Dismissed 9/23/56 |
| SO, Birmingham, Alabama | FRANK LEE MORRIS #32035 | 9/22/56 | Federal theft | turned over to USM |
| U.S. Penitentiary, Atlanta, Georgia | FRANK LEE MORRIS #77735 | 9/23/56 | Burglary of Federal Deposit Ins. Corp. bank | 14 years |
| U.S. Penitentiary, Alcatraz, Calif. | FRANK LEE MORRIS #1441-AZ | 1/18/60 | Burglary of FDIC bank | |

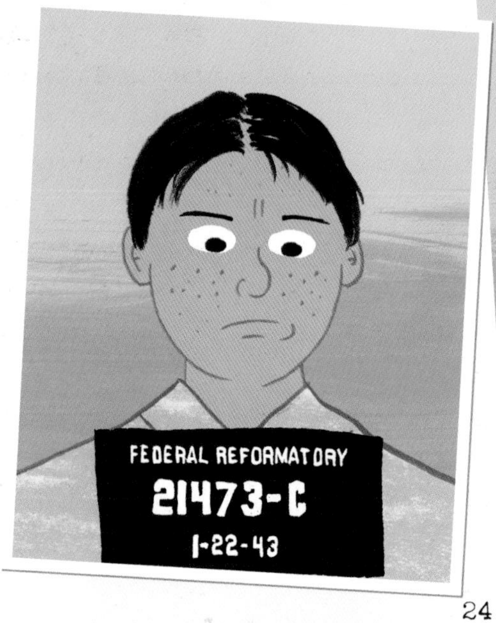
FEDERAL REFORMATORY
21473-C
1-22-43

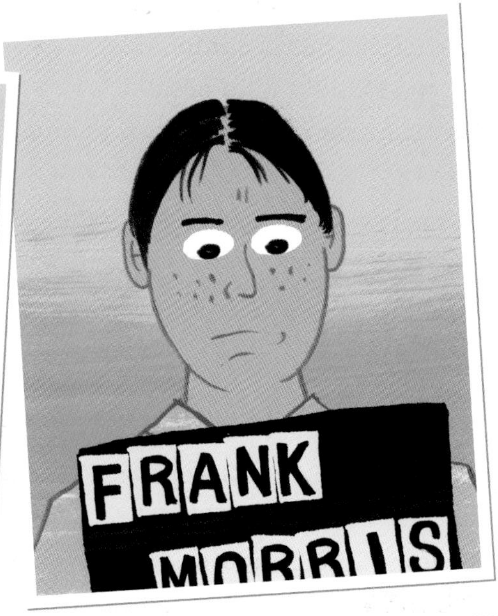
FRANK
MORRIS

# PART FOUR:
# LUCKY NUMBER THIRTEEN

USPA 77796 9 21 56

Born in WASHINGTON, DC, in 1926 to a teenage runaway, FRANK LEE MORRIS was placed in foster care when he was just six months old. He saw his mother occasionally, but she abandoned him completely by the age of six, and it is presumed that she died shortly thereafter. By the age of thirteen he himself had become a runaway and was convicted of burglary in WEST VIRGINIA.

MORRIS spent the remainder of his teenage years breaking the law, getting caught, being incarcerated, and then escaping from wherever he was being detained. Eventually his crimes evolved from small-time misdemeanors to full-scale felonies, and in 1955 he was sentenced to ten years in the LOUISIANA STATE PENITENTIARY for armed robbery and possession of marijuana. But while working a detail harvesting sugarcane, MORRIS escaped. He lay low for a few months, but after robbing a bank in KANSAS CITY, MORRIS was nabbed by the FBI and sentenced to fourteen years, to be served at the federal prison in ATLANTA.

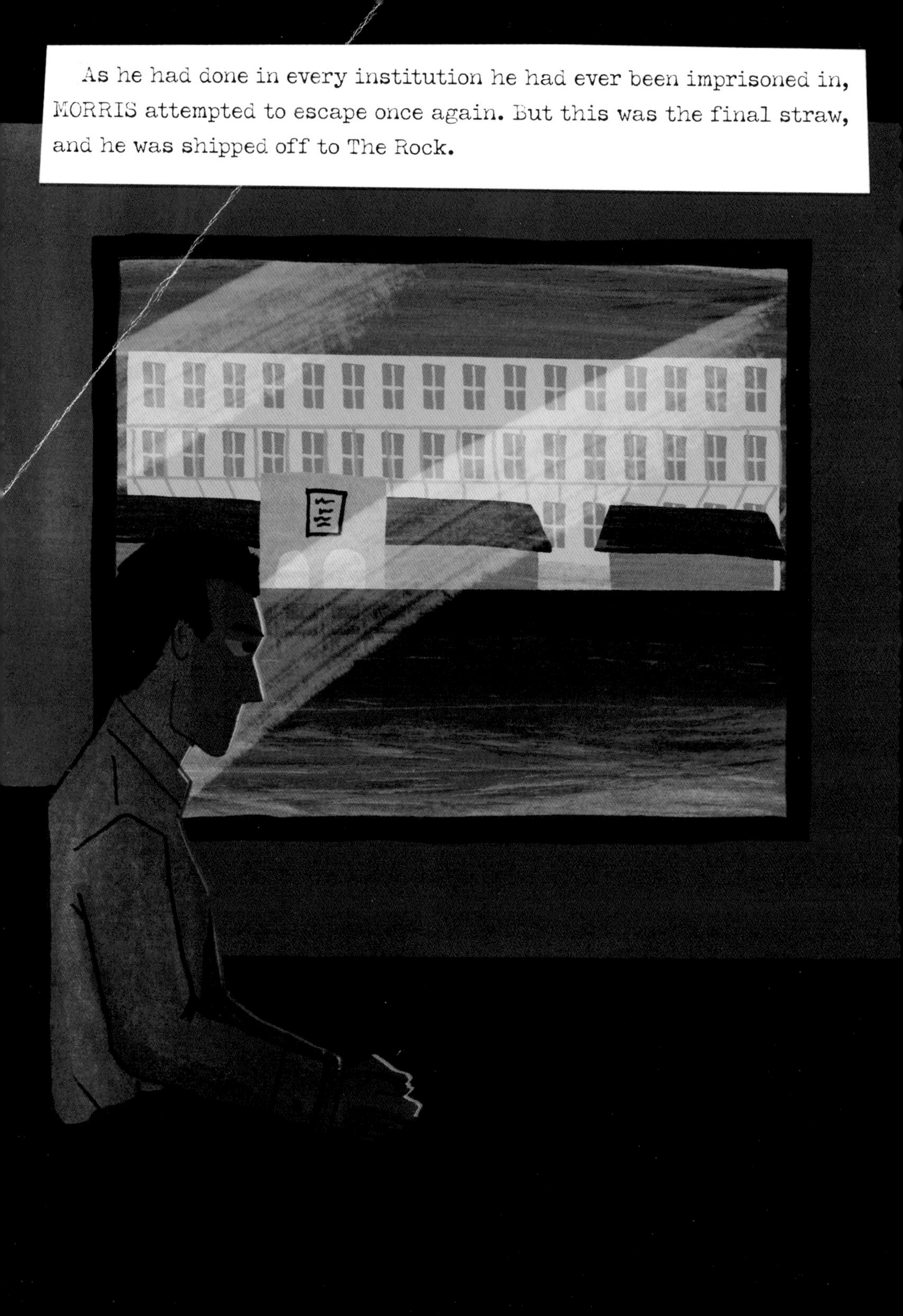
As he had done in every institution he had ever been imprisoned in, MORRIS attempted to escape once again. But this was the final straw, and he was shipped off to The Rock.

On January 18, 1960, MORRIS stepped off the ferry and onto Alcatraz Island. Fittingly, on his official admittance paperwork, FRANK MORRIS'S occupation was listed as "escape artist."

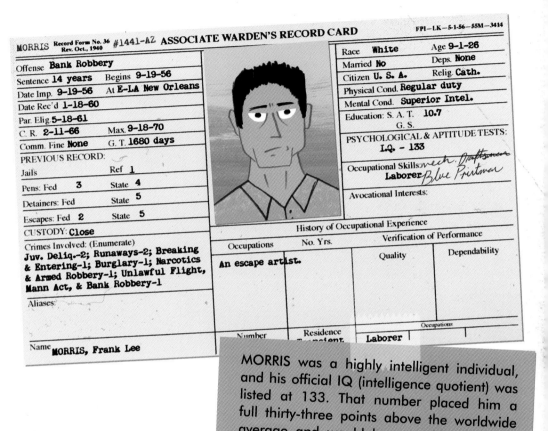

| MORRIS Record Form No. 36 Rev. Oct., 1940 #1441-AZ ASSOCIATE WARDEN'S RECORD CARD | | | | FPI—LK—5-1-56—55M—3414 |
|---|---|---|---|---|

Offense **Bank Robbery**
Sentence **14 years**  Begins **9-19-56**
Date Imp. **9-19-56**  At **E-LA New Orleans**
Date Rec'd **1-18-60**
Par. Elig. **5-18-61**
C. R. **2-11-66**  Max. **9-18-70**
Comm. Fine **None**  G. T. **1680 days**
PREVIOUS RECORD:
Jails  Ref **1**
Pens: Fed **3**  State **4**
Detainers: Fed  State **5**
Escapes: Fed **2**  State **5**
CUSTODY: **Close**
Crimes Involved: (Enumerate)
**Juv. Deliq.-2; Runaways-2; Breaking & Entering-1; Burglary-1; Narcotics & Armed Robbery-1; Unlawful Flight, Mann Act, & Bank Robbery-1**
Aliases:
Name **MORRIS, Frank Lee**

Race **White**  Age **9-1-26**
Married **No**  Deps. **None**
Citizen **U. S. A.**  Relig. **Cath.**
Physical Cond. **Regular duty**
Mental Cond. **Superior Intel.**
Education: S. A. T. **10.7**  G. S.
PSYCHOLOGICAL & APTITUDE TESTS:
I.Q. - **133**
Occupational Skills: *mech. Draftsman* Laborer *Blue Printman*
Avocational Interests:

History of Occupational Experience

| Occupations | No. Yrs. | Verification of Performance | |
|---|---|---|---|
| | | Quality | Dependability |
| **An escape artist.** | | | |
| | | | |

| Number | Residence Transient. | Laborer | Occupations |
|---|---|---|---|

MORRIS was a highly intelligent individual, and his official IQ (intelligence quotient) was listed at 133. That number placed him a full thirty-three points above the worldwide average and would have qualified him for membership in Mensa (a high-IQ society open to individuals who place in the ninety-eighth percentile on standardized IQ tests).

As all new prisoners did, MORRIS spent his first thirty days on Alcatraz quarantined in C block, getting acclimated to what would be his home for the next decade, or six years with good behavior.

MORRIS was eventually assigned to cell 138 in B block, right next to ALLEN WEST in cell 140, setting in motion the greatest prison escape the world had ever seen.

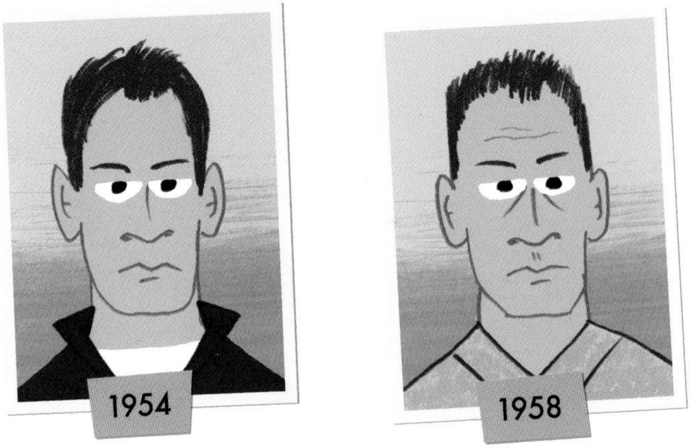
1954
1958

ALLEN CLAYTON WEST was serving his second stint at Alcatraz, this time for transporting stolen vehicles across state lines. WEST had been assigned a work detail painting the walls and ceiling in the area on top of the cell blocks.

WEST was prepping the area to be painted when he noticed that one of the old ventilators in the ceiling remained intact. There were still bars running across the intake hole, but it had not been cemented shut, like the rest of the decommissioned vents.

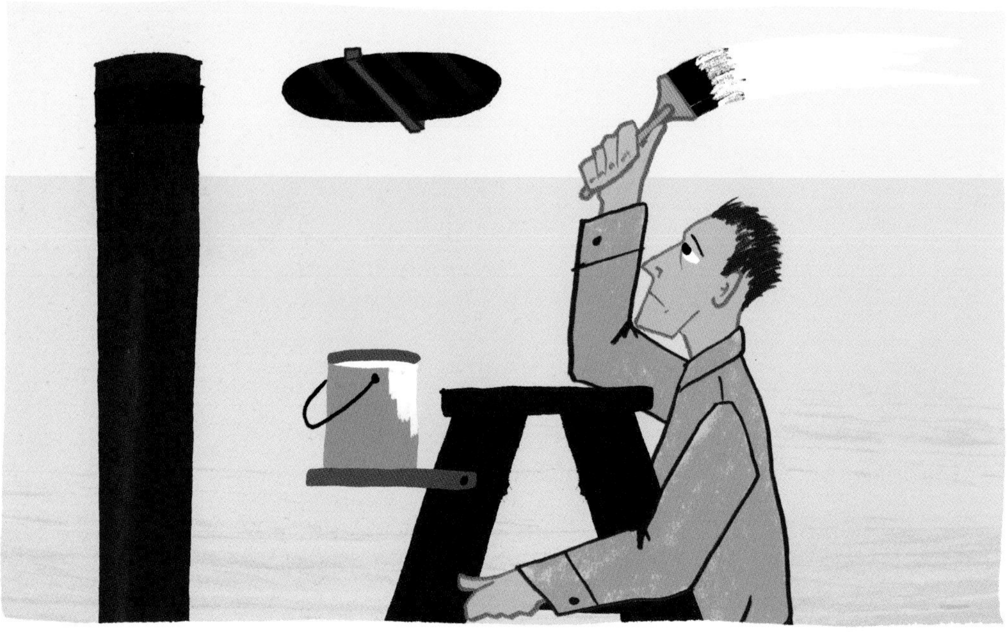

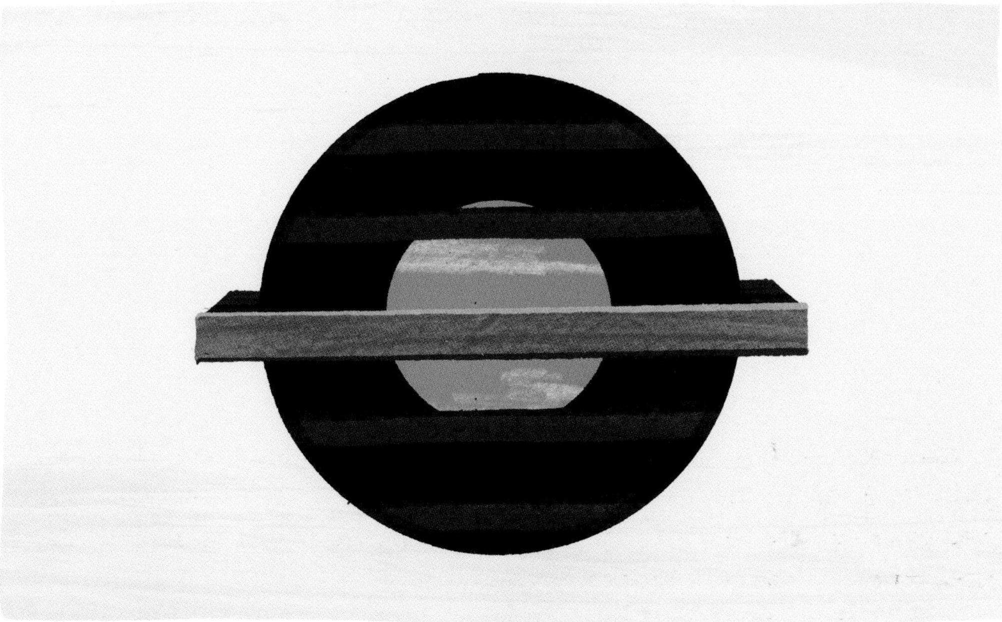

This meant that there might be a way to get up to the roof of the cell house. WEST also discovered an air duct that ran from the roof all the way down the side of the building to the ground.

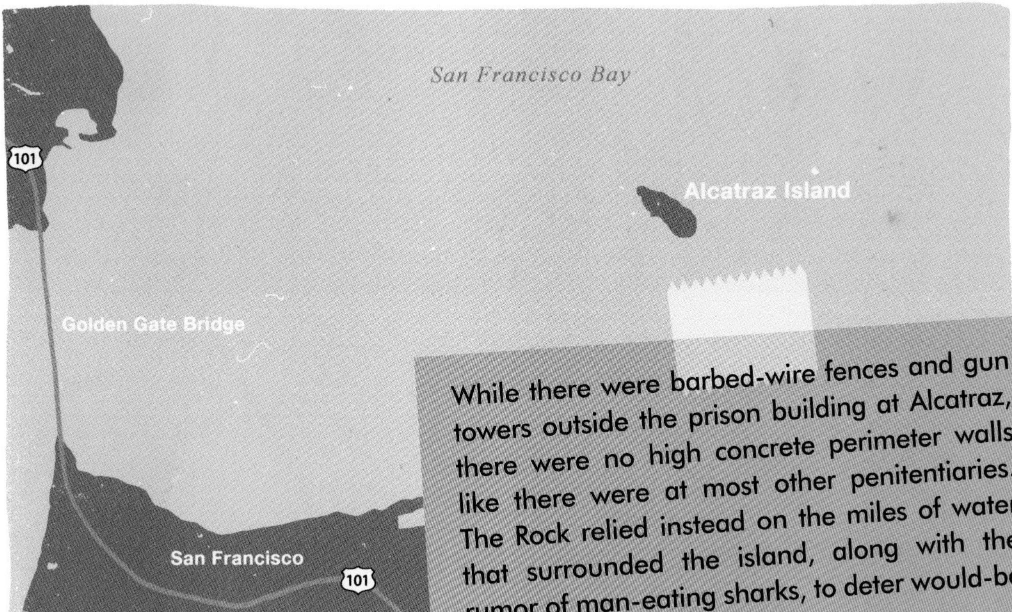
San Francisco Bay
101
Alcatraz Island
Golden Gate Bridge
San Francisco
101

While there were barbed-wire fences and gun towers outside the prison building at Alcatraz, there were no high concrete perimeter walls like there were at most other penitentiaries. The Rock relied instead on the miles of water that surrounded the island, along with the rumor of man-eating sharks, to deter would-be escapees.

As a cost-cutting measure, Alcatraz didn't have a freshwater sewer system, and years of salt water in the plumbing had caused the pipes to rust and erode. Around the time WEST discovered the decommissioned vent to the roof, plumbers were called in to do some maintenance work in the utility corridor.

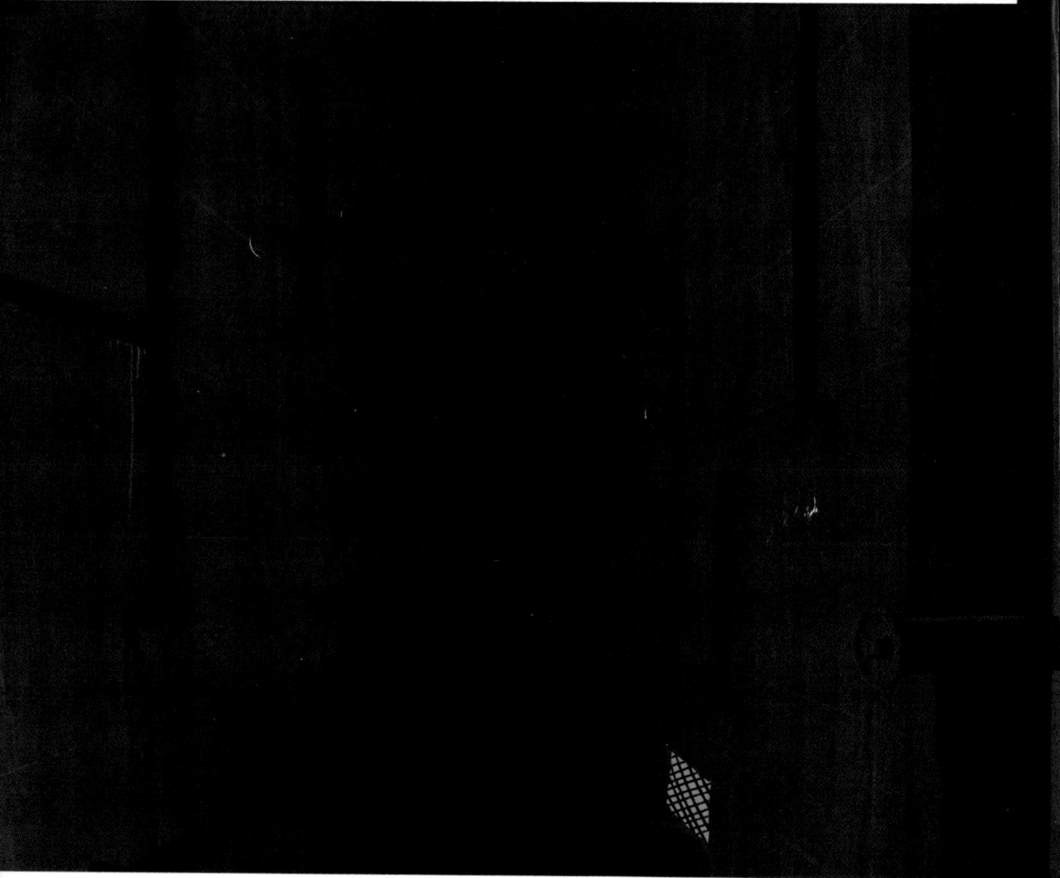

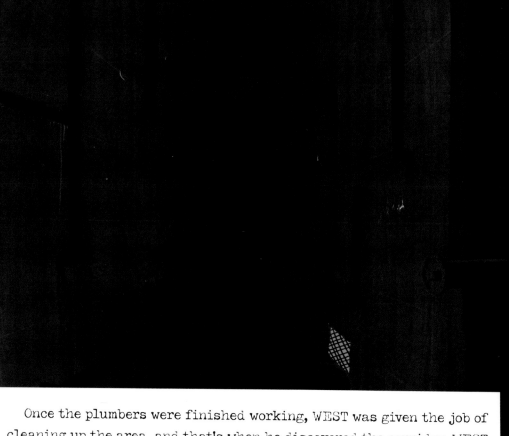

Once the plumbers were finished working, WEST was given the job of cleaning up the area, and that's when he discovered the corridor. WEST figured that if he could get himself into the utility corridor from his cell, he could climb up the pipes to the top of the cell block. From there he could make his way through the decommissioned vent in the ceiling, up onto the roof, and then down the side of the building. The only thing stopping him then would be the SAN FRANCISCO BAY.

Each cell block had two rows of cells separated by a three-foot-wide utility corridor. The narrow corridors ran the whole length and the entire three-story height of the cell blocks and contained a mishmash of pipes and air vents.

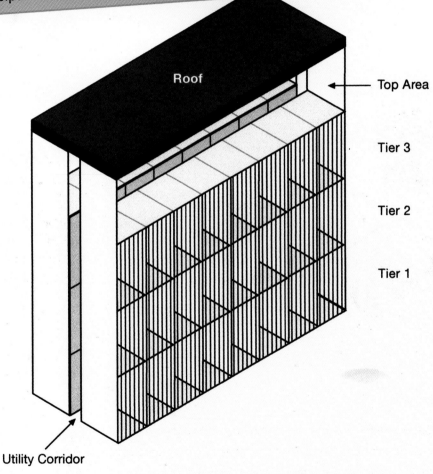

Roof

Top Area

Tier 3

Tier 2

Tier 1

Utility Corridor

ALLEN WEST had discovered a way out, but in order to pull off an escape from Alcatraz, he'd need some help from people he could trust.

JOHN ANGLIN had previously served time with ALLEN WEST in FLORIDA, and coincidentally he also knew FRANK MORRIS from his time incarcerated in Atlanta. He was currently five cells down from WEST, in cell 150, next to his brother, CLARENCE ANGLIN, who was in cell 152.

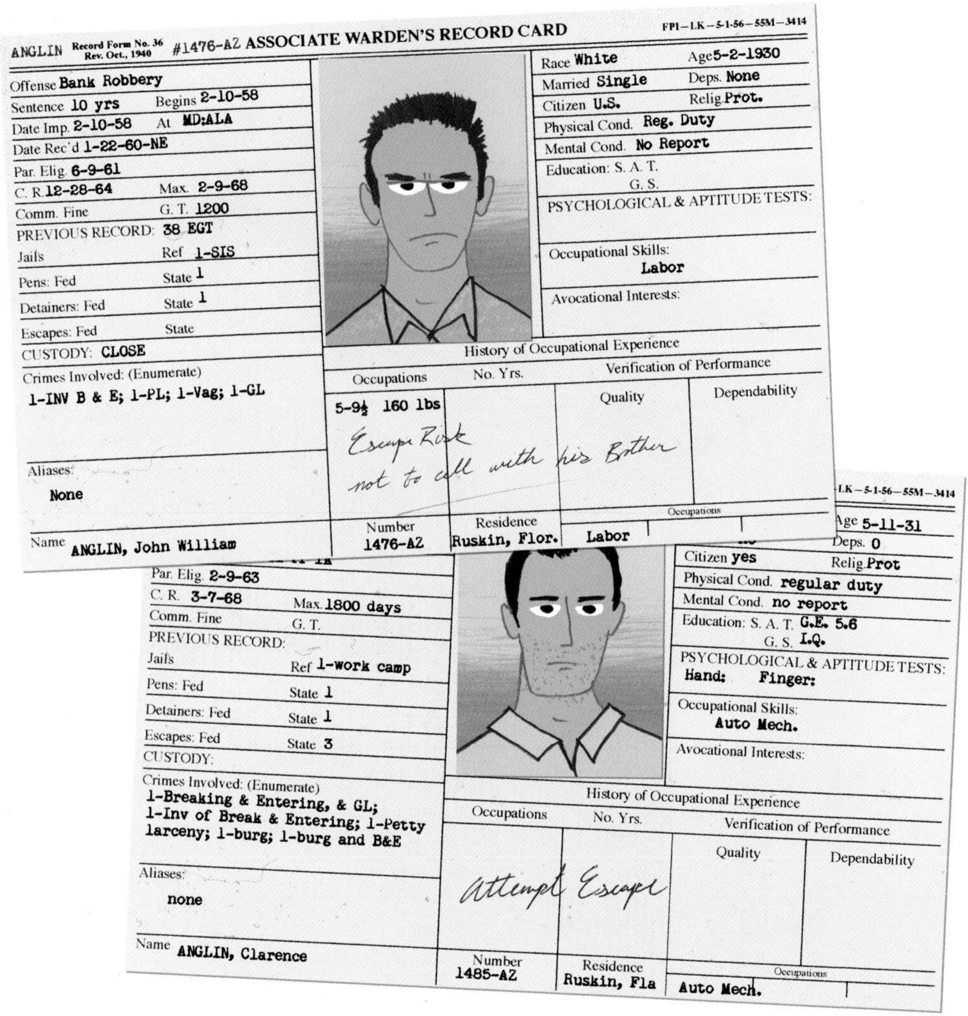

ANGLIN Record Form No. 36 Rev. Oct., 1940 #1476-AZ ASSOCIATE WARDEN'S RECORD CARD FPI—LK—5-1-56—55M—3414

Offense Bank Robbery
Sentence 10 yrs Begins 2-10-58
Date Imp. 2-10-58 At MD:ALA
Date Rec'd 1-22-60-NE
Par. Elig. 6-9-61
C. R. 12-28-64 Max. 2-9-68
Comm. Fine G. T. 1200
PREVIOUS RECORD: 38 EGT
Jails Ref 1-SIS
Pens: Fed State 1
Detainers: Fed State 1
Escapes: Fed State
CUSTODY: CLOSE
Crimes Involved: (Enumerate)
1-INV B & E; 1-PL; 1-Vag; 1-GL
Aliases:
None
Name ANGLIN, John William

Race White Age 5-2-1930
Married Single Deps. None
Citizen U.S. Relig. Prot.
Physical Cond. Reg. Duty
Mental Cond. No Report
Education: S. A. T.
G. S.
PSYCHOLOGICAL & APTITUDE TESTS:
Occupational Skills:
Labor
Avocational Interests:
History of Occupational Experience
Occupations No. Yrs. Verification of Performance
Quality Dependability
5-9½ 160 lbs
Escape Risk
not to cell with his Brother
Number 1476-AZ Residence Ruskin, Flor. Occupations Labor

LK—5-1-56—55M—3414
Age 5-11-31
Deps. 0
Citizen yes Relig. Prot
Physical Cond. regular duty
Mental Cond. no report
Education: S. A. T. G.E. 5.6
G. S. I.Q.
PSYCHOLOGICAL & APTITUDE TESTS:
Hand: Finger:
Occupational Skills:
Auto Mech.
Avocational Interests:
History of Occupational Experience
Occupations No. Yrs. Verification of Performance
Quality Dependability
attempt Escape

Par. Elig. 2-9-63
C. R. 3-7-68 Max. 1800 days
Comm. Fine G. T.
PREVIOUS RECORD:
Jails Ref 1-work camp
Pens: Fed State 1
Detainers: Fed State 1
Escapes: Fed State 3
CUSTODY:
Crimes Involved: (Enumerate)
1-Breaking & Entering, & GL;
1-Inv of Break & Entering; 1-Petty larceny; 1-burg; 1-burg and B&E
Aliases:
none
Name ANGLIN, Clarence
Number 1485-AZ Residence Ruskin, Fla Occupations Auto Mech.

The ANGLINS, who were initially sentenced for bank robbery, had been sent to Alcatraz after a botched escape attempt from the UNITED STATES PENITENTIARY, LEAVENWORTH, in KANSAS. Although it was recommended that the brothers be separated, the warden at the time felt that it was good for morale for siblings to be celled next to each other.

In the twenty-seven years since Alcatraz had first begun operating as a federal penitentiary, the strict nature in which it governed its prisoners had begun to relax. When Warden JOHNSTON first opened the prison in 1934, communication between prisoners was strictly forbidden. In the mess hall, inmates used to sit on one side of long cafeteria tables, and they only had twenty minutes to eat. If you spoke or didn't finish your meal, you were thrown into "the hole."

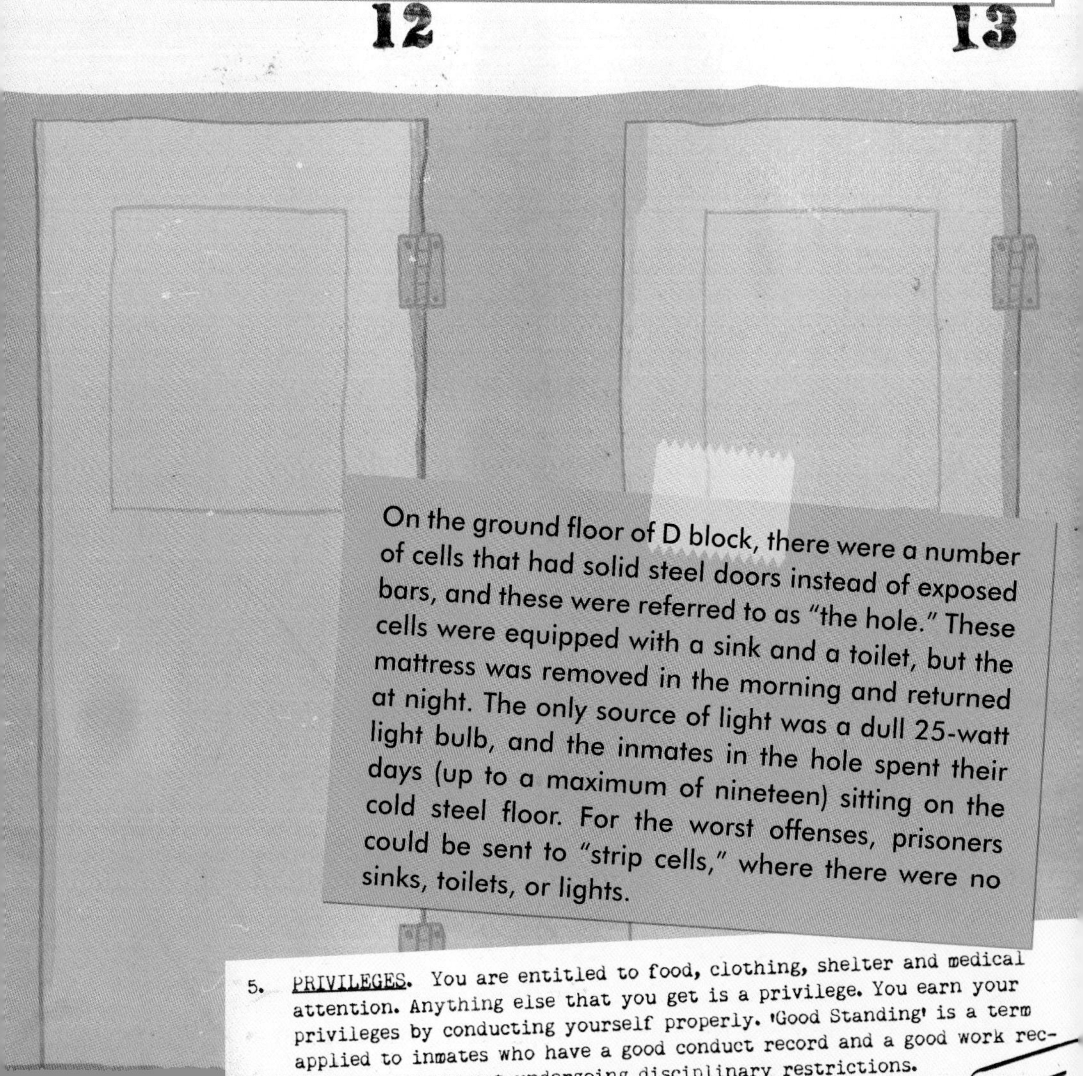

12
13


On the ground floor of D block, there were a number of cells that had solid steel doors instead of exposed bars, and these were referred to as "the hole." These cells were equipped with a sink and a toilet, but the mattress was removed in the morning and returned at night. The only source of light was a dull 25-watt light bulb, and the inmates in the hole spent their days (up to a maximum of nineteen) sitting on the cold steel floor. For the worst offenses, prisoners could be sent to "strip cells," where there were no sinks, toilets, or lights.

5. <u>PRIVILEGES</u>. You are entitled to food, clothing, shelter and medical attention. Anything else that you get is a privilege. You earn your privileges by conducting yourself properly. 'Good Standing' is a term applied to inmates who have a good conduct record and a good work record and who are not undergoing disciplinary restrictions.

6. <u>DISCIPLINARY ACTION</u> may result in loss of some or all of your privileges and/or confinement in the Treatment Unit.

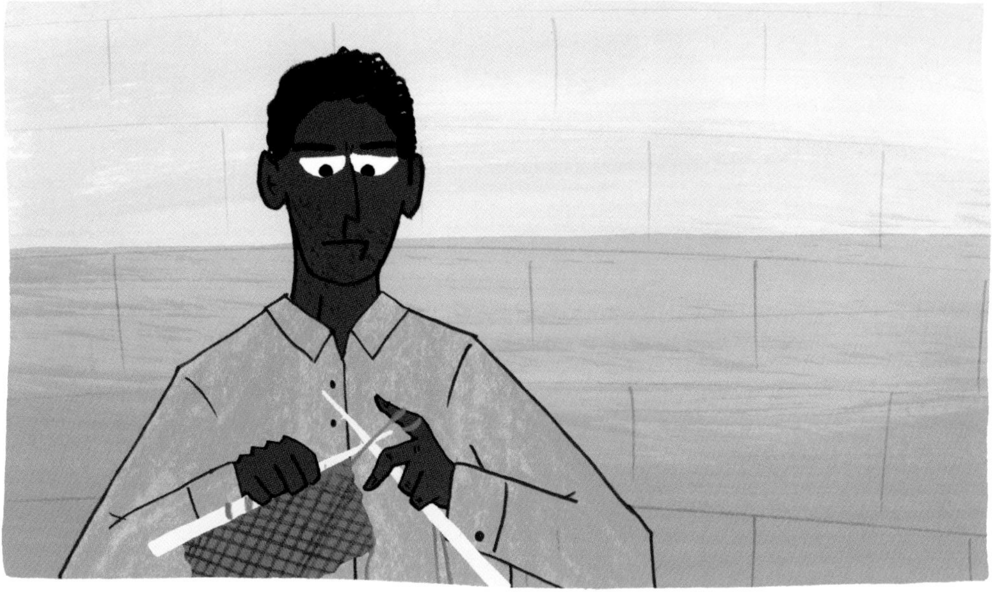

The prison had earned its nickname "Hellcatraz." But after allegations of human rights violations against prisoners, policies changed. Inmates were now permitted to have conversations with their neighbors, knit (albeit with plastic needles), and play musical instruments in the evenings.

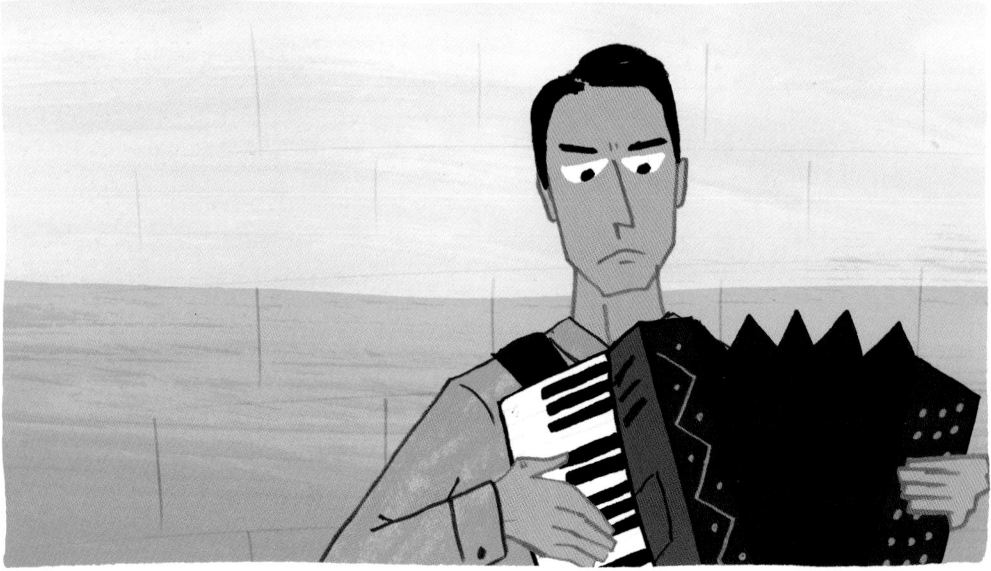

The long tables in the mess hall were removed to make way for smaller ones where inmates could talk during their meals. It was at one of these very tables that ALLEN WEST and the ANGLINS let MORRIS in on their plan to escape. But before they could even think about scaling the pipes in the utility corridor and climbing up through a ventilator shaft to the roof, they'd have to figure out how to escape from their cells.

As it turned out, all they'd need for that was to practice routine personal hygiene.

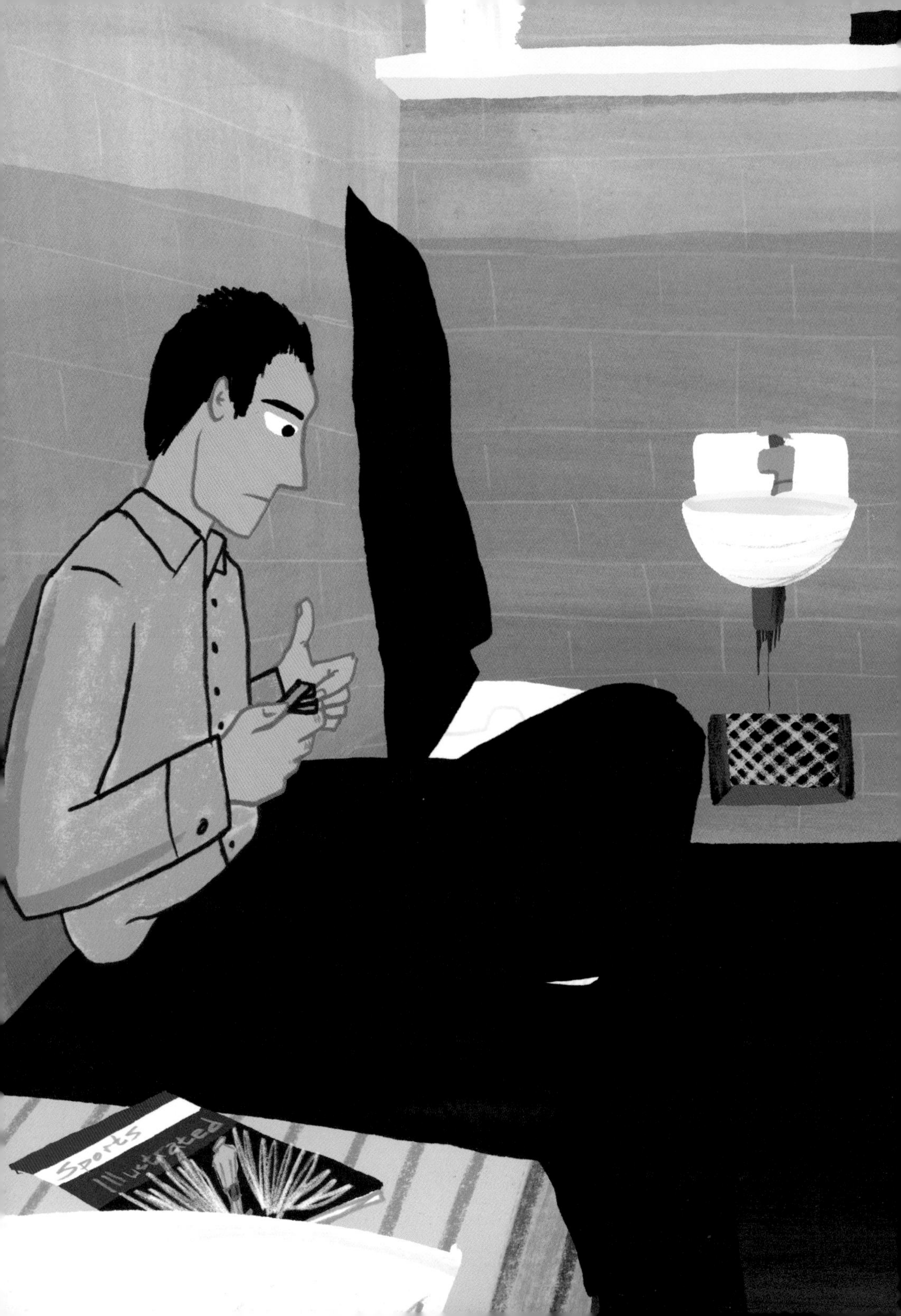
Sports
Illustrated

# PART FIVE:
# PRISON INGENUITY

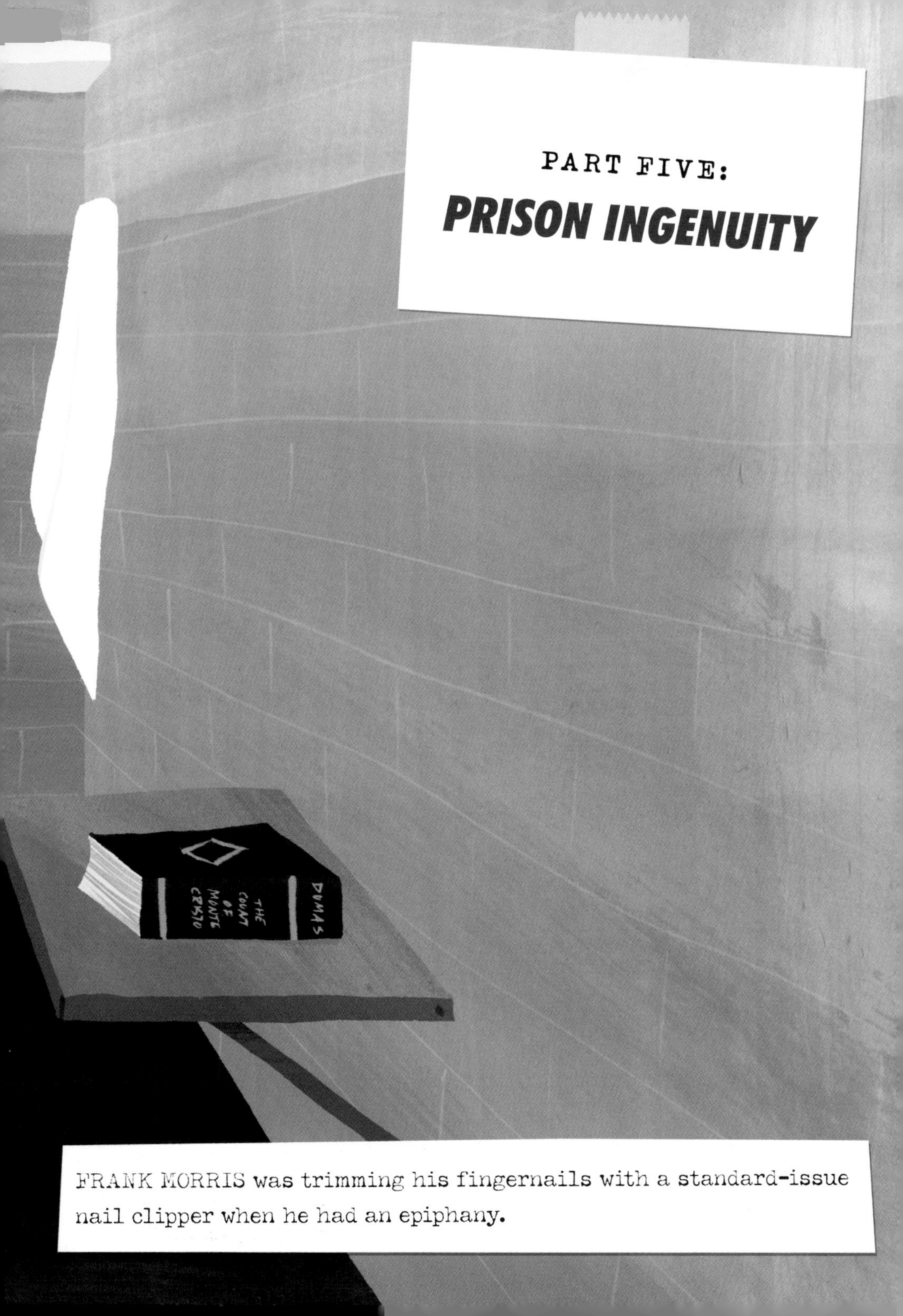
THE COUNT OF MONTE CRISTO
DUMAS

FRANK MORRIS was trimming his fingernails with a standard-issue nail clipper when he had an epiphany.

The nail clippers had a small file on a swinging hinge, similar to that of a Swiss Army knife. Where most people might have seen a simple nail file, MORRIS saw a potential digging tool.

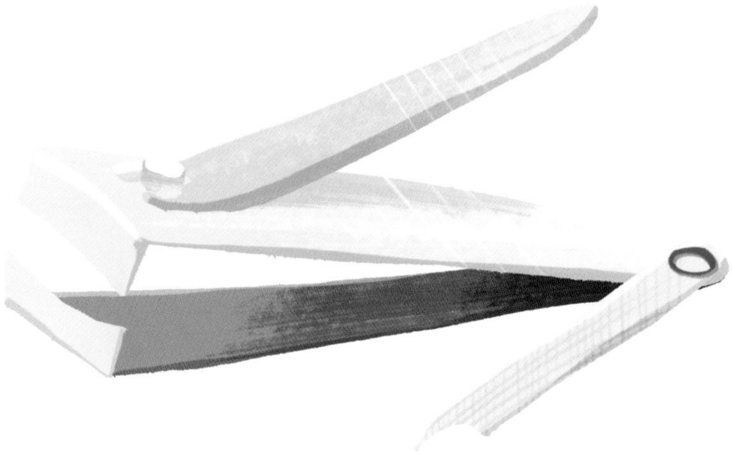

He knelt on the floor and examined the 6 x 10-inch metal ventilation grill that was on the back wall of every cell, and peering through the grate, he could see right into the utility corridor. The larger obstacle, of course, would be the 8-inch-thick concrete wall that surrounded the vent.

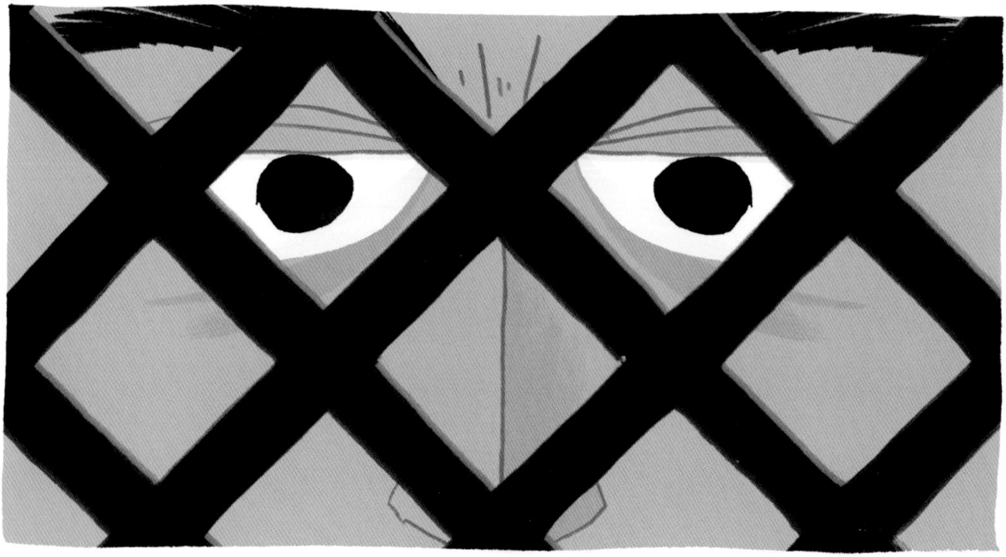

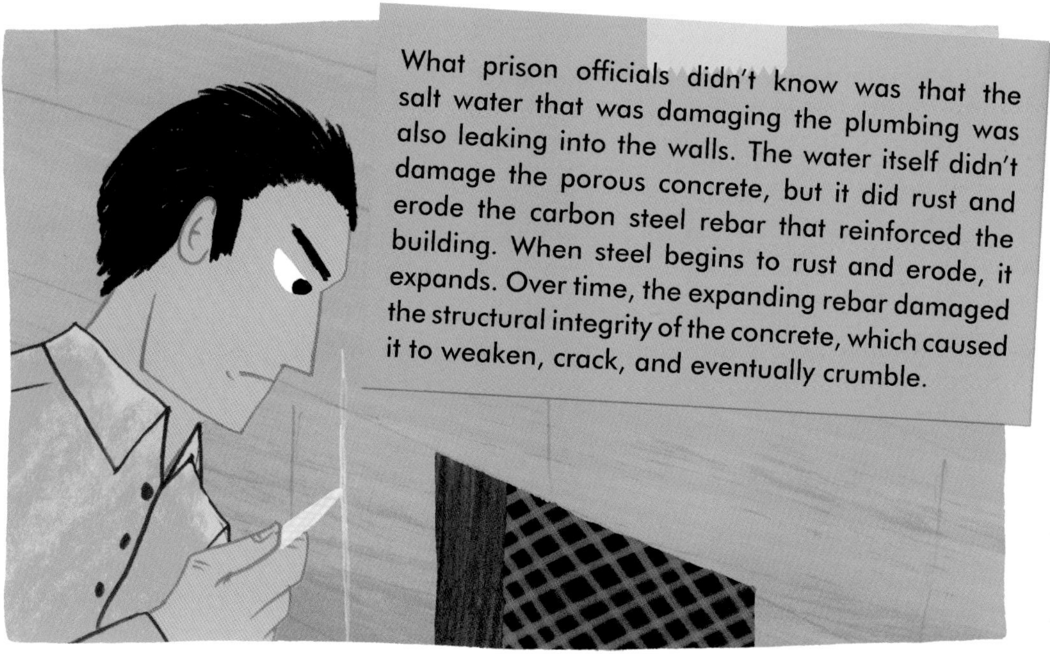
What prison officials didn't know was that the salt water that was damaging the plumbing was also leaking into the walls. The water itself didn't damage the porous concrete, but it did rust and erode the carbon steel rebar that reinforced the building. When steel begins to rust and erode, it expands. Over time, the expanding rebar damaged the structural integrity of the concrete, which caused it to weaken, crack, and eventually crumble.

MORRIS scratched the nail file against the wall and was surprised to see particles of concrete fall to the floor. MORRIS swept up the concrete dust and, using a dampened handkerchief, smoothed it back into the scratch mark like plaster. He examined his handiwork, and was pleased to see that the wall looked completely undisturbed.

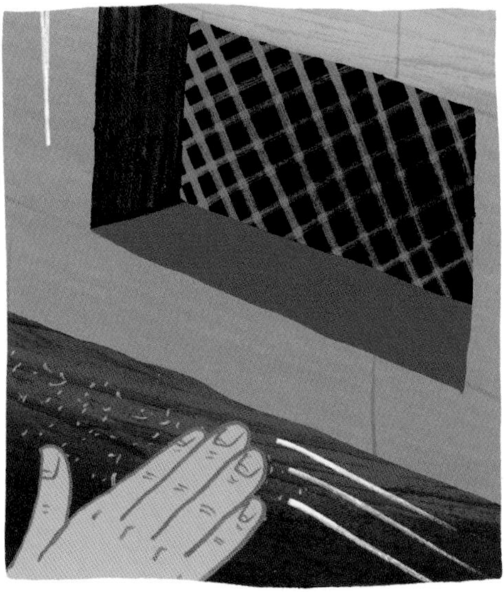

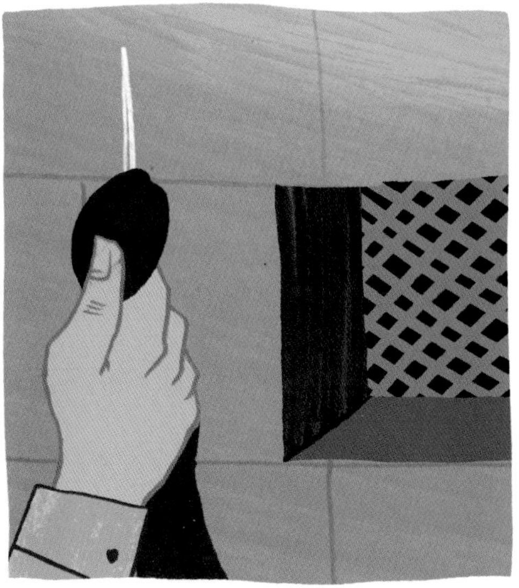

From their own cells, JOHN ANGLIN and FRANK MORRIS began the arduous task of digging through the 8-inch concrete wall with whatever tools they could find, while their neighbors acted as lookouts. CLARENCE would watch his brother JOHN'S back, while ALLEN WEST would watch MORRIS'S. That way, once MORRIS and JOHN ANGLIN were finished digging out, WEST and CLARENCE could learn from the others' previous mistakes and move along at a more streamlined pace.

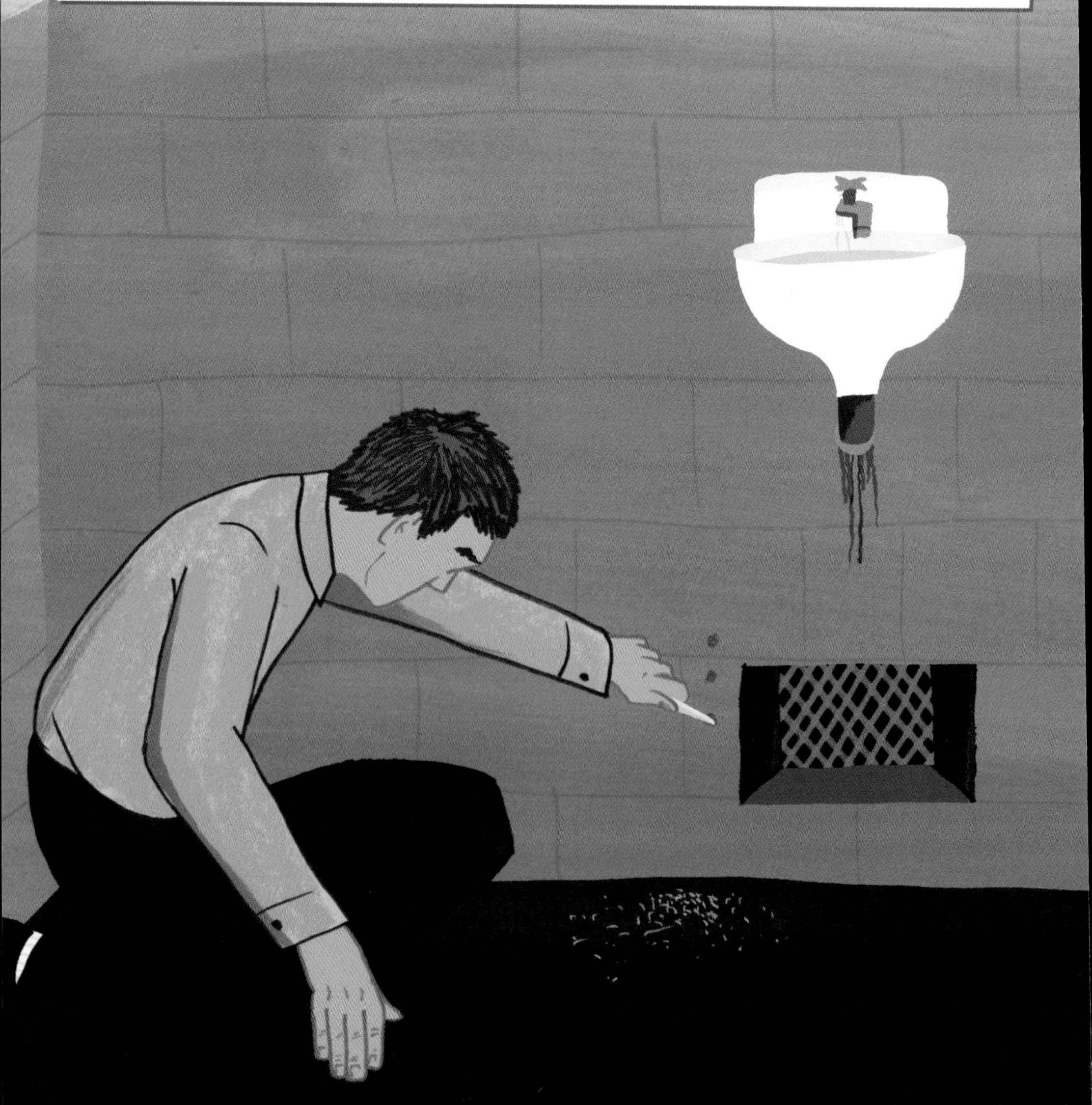

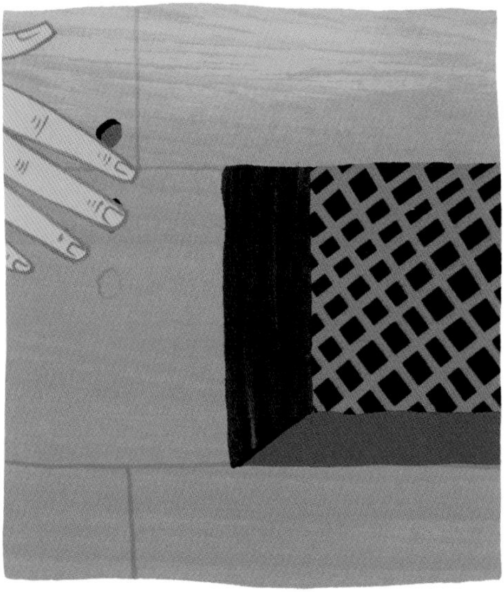

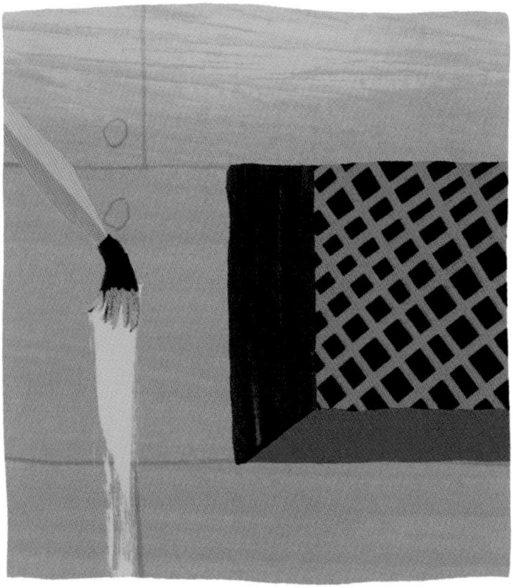

The plan was simple: They dug small holes around the perimeter of the vent's grill, and once they had drilled a hole all the way through the wall, they filled it in with a mixture of soap and concrete dust. The remaining concrete dust was flushed down the sink, and any larger pieces were smuggled outside in the men's pockets. Then, using paint sets that CLARENCE purchased through the prison's commissary, they painted over their progress.

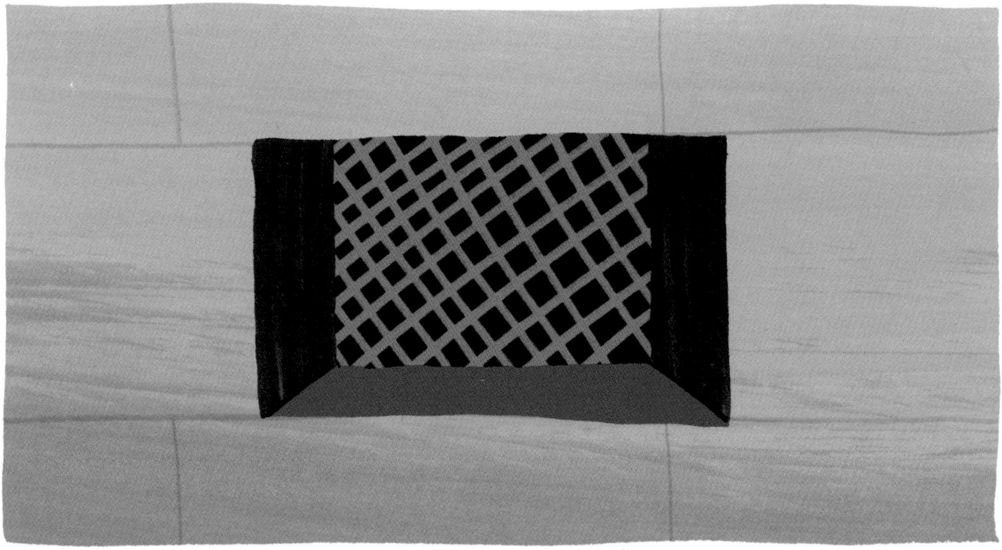

Digging through 8 inches of concrete with a nail file for four hours a night was beginning to take its toll. JOHN ANGLIN was digging with a sharpened spoon he had smuggled out of the mess hall, so MORRIS thought he'd try the same, but that still wasn't efficient enough. He needed to figure out a way to fasten the nail file to the more ergonomic and comfortable handle of the spoon, and that's when FRANK MORRIS came up with the idea of brazing.

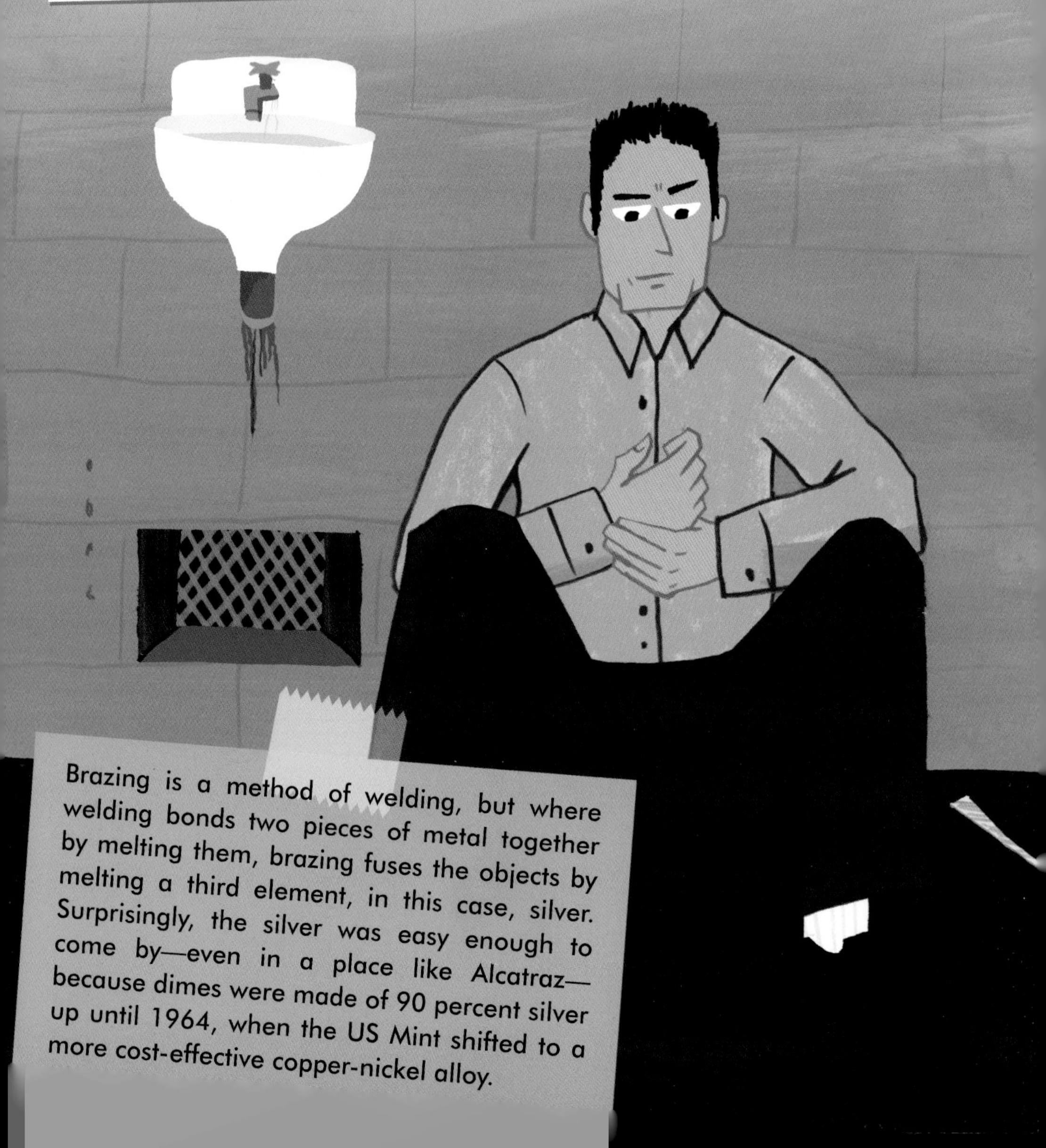

Brazing is a method of welding, but where welding bonds two pieces of metal together by melting them, brazing fuses the objects by melting a third element, in this case, silver. Surprisingly, the silver was easy enough to come by—even in a place like Alcatraz—because dimes were made of 90 percent silver up until 1964, when the US Mint shifted to a more cost-effective copper-nickel alloy.

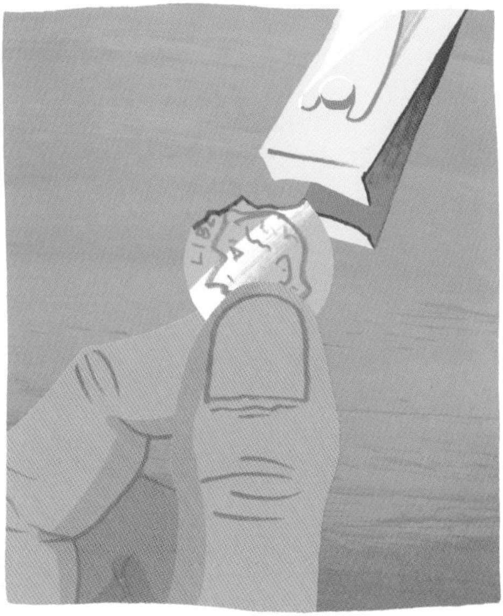

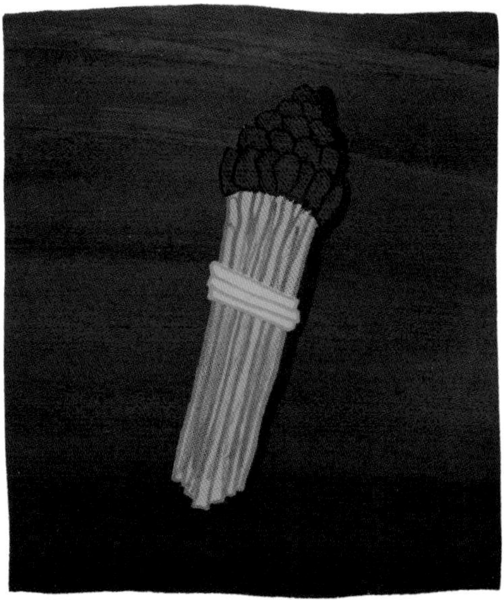

Using the nail clippers, MORRIS shaved the dime into tiny fragments, which he placed on the top of a spoon handle. He then banded matches into a bundle and melted the silver. Finally he placed the nail file onto the melted silver, which fused it to the spoon, creating a pick.

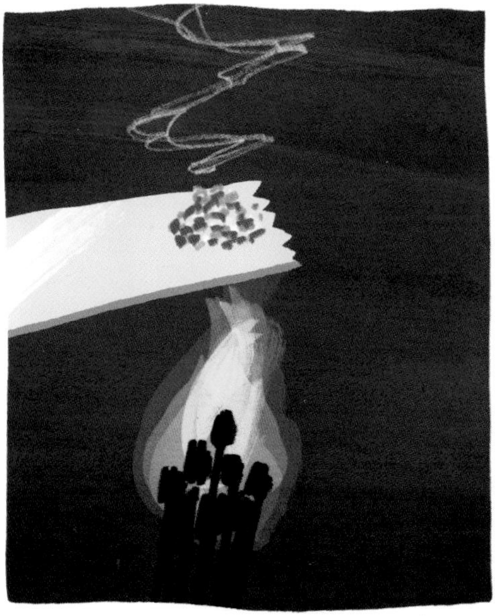

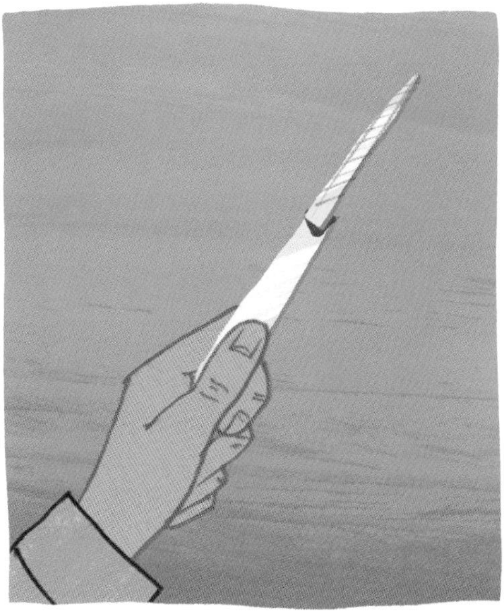

Soon MORRIS and JOHN ANGLIN had made their way around the perimeter of the ventilator grills, and now had holes that were way too big for soap and concrete dust to patch up. That's when CLARENCE ANGLIN had the idea to take shredded magazine pages, soap, concrete dust, water, and glue that FRANK MORRIS had smuggled from his work detail assignment in the brush shop, and make papier-mâché.

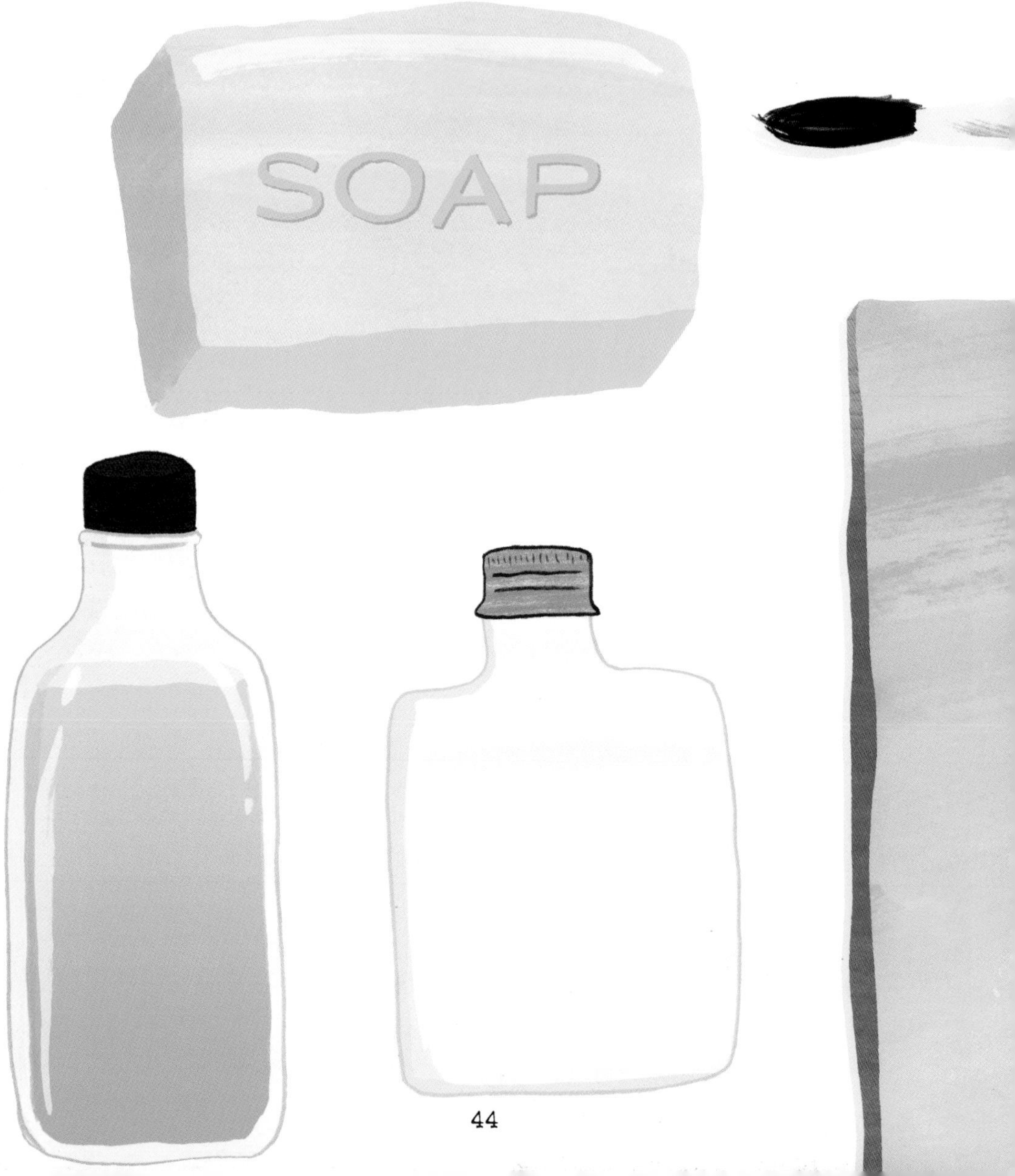
SOAP

CLARENCE combined the mixture into a pulp in his sink, and then flattened it into a rectangle. After it had dried into a stiff board, he traced and cut the same pattern that was on the ventilator grill, and painted it to match the wall. He even created larger sections to act as a false wall surrounding the grate.

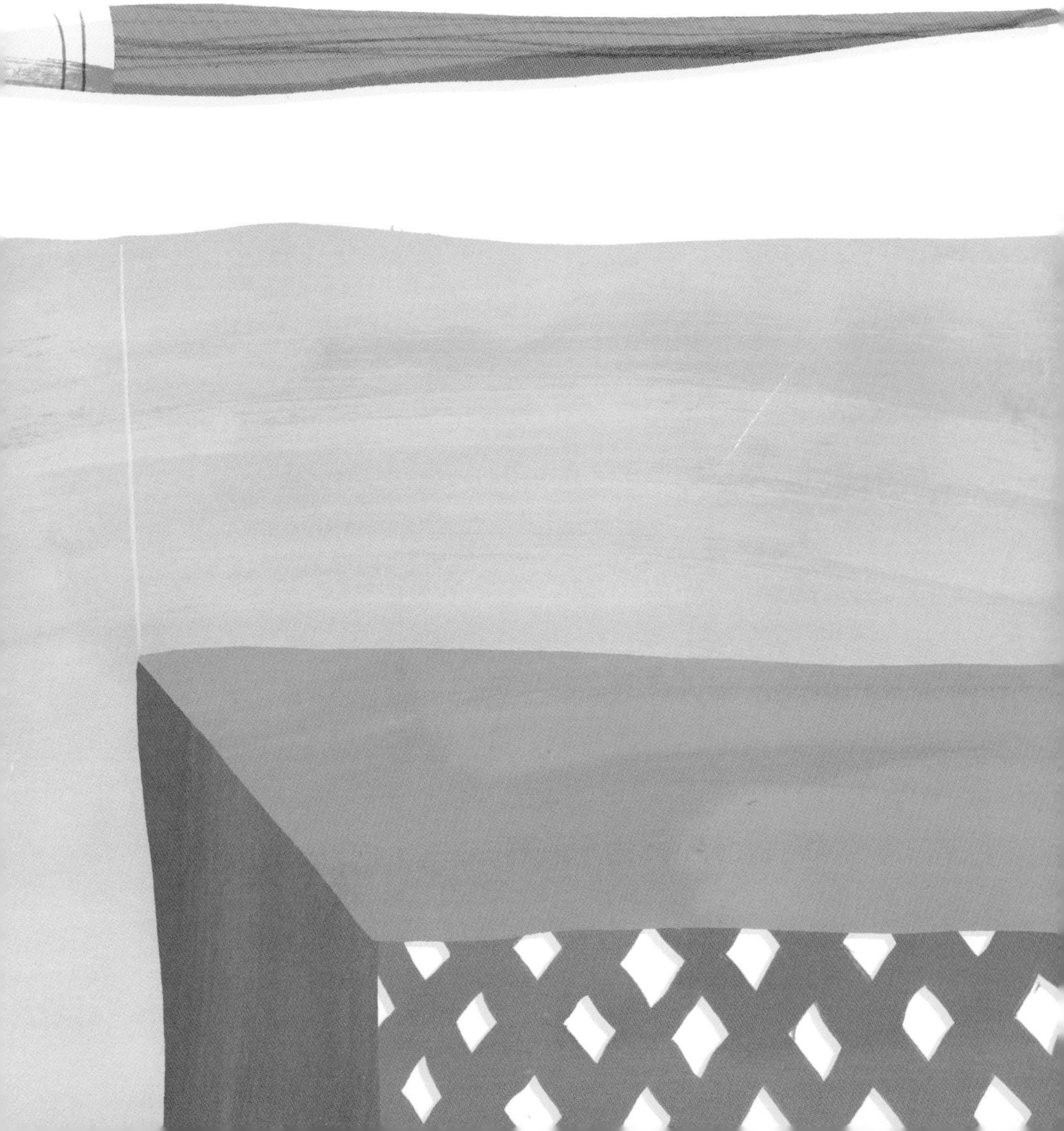

Once FRANK MORRIS and JOHN ANGLIN finished digging their holes, it was time for CLARENCE ANGLIN and ALLEN WEST to begin. They had the tools and cardboard vent coverings ready to go, and in order to speed things up, JOHN ANGLIN even snuck into the utility corridor to dig out CLARENCE'S wall from the back.

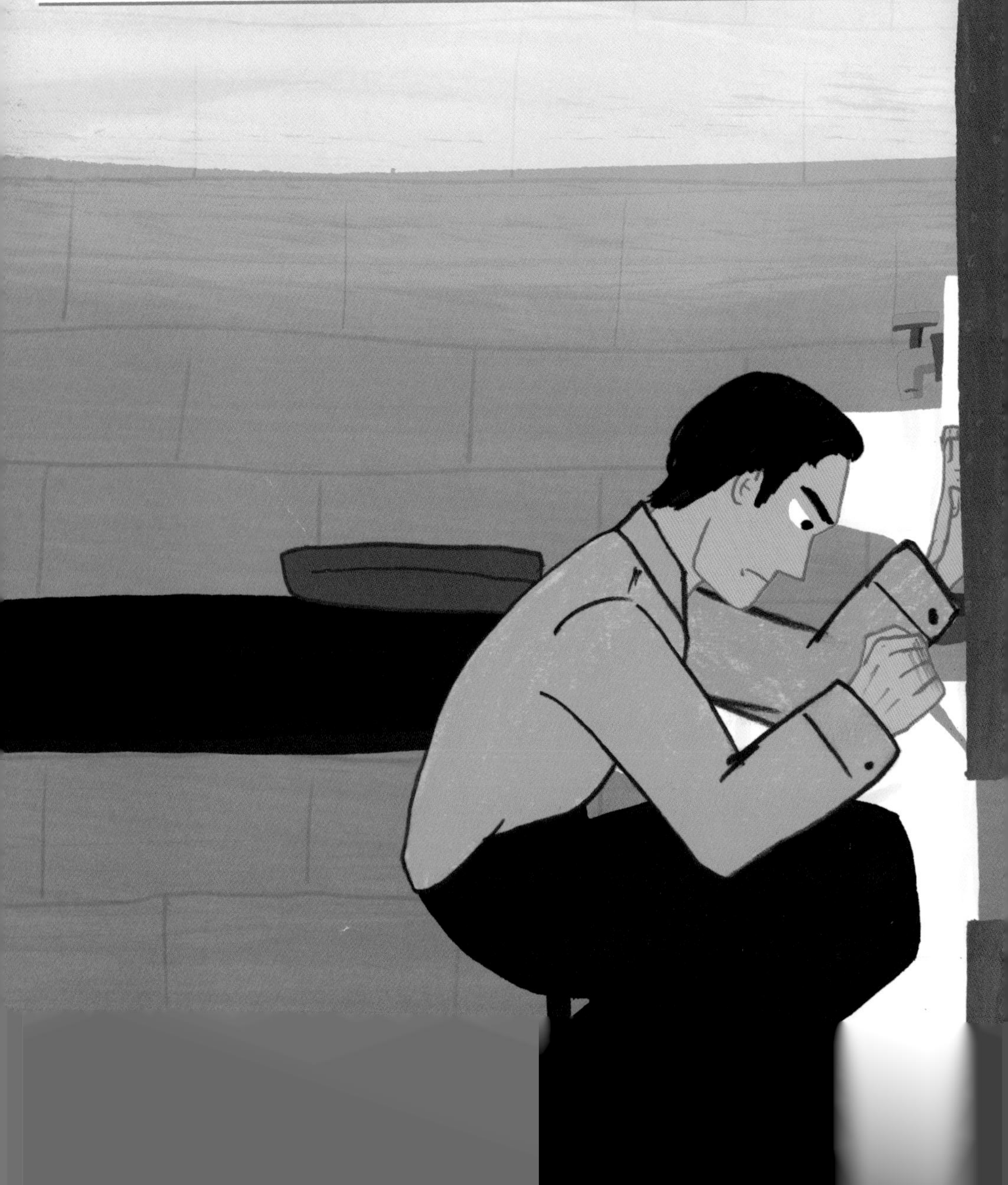

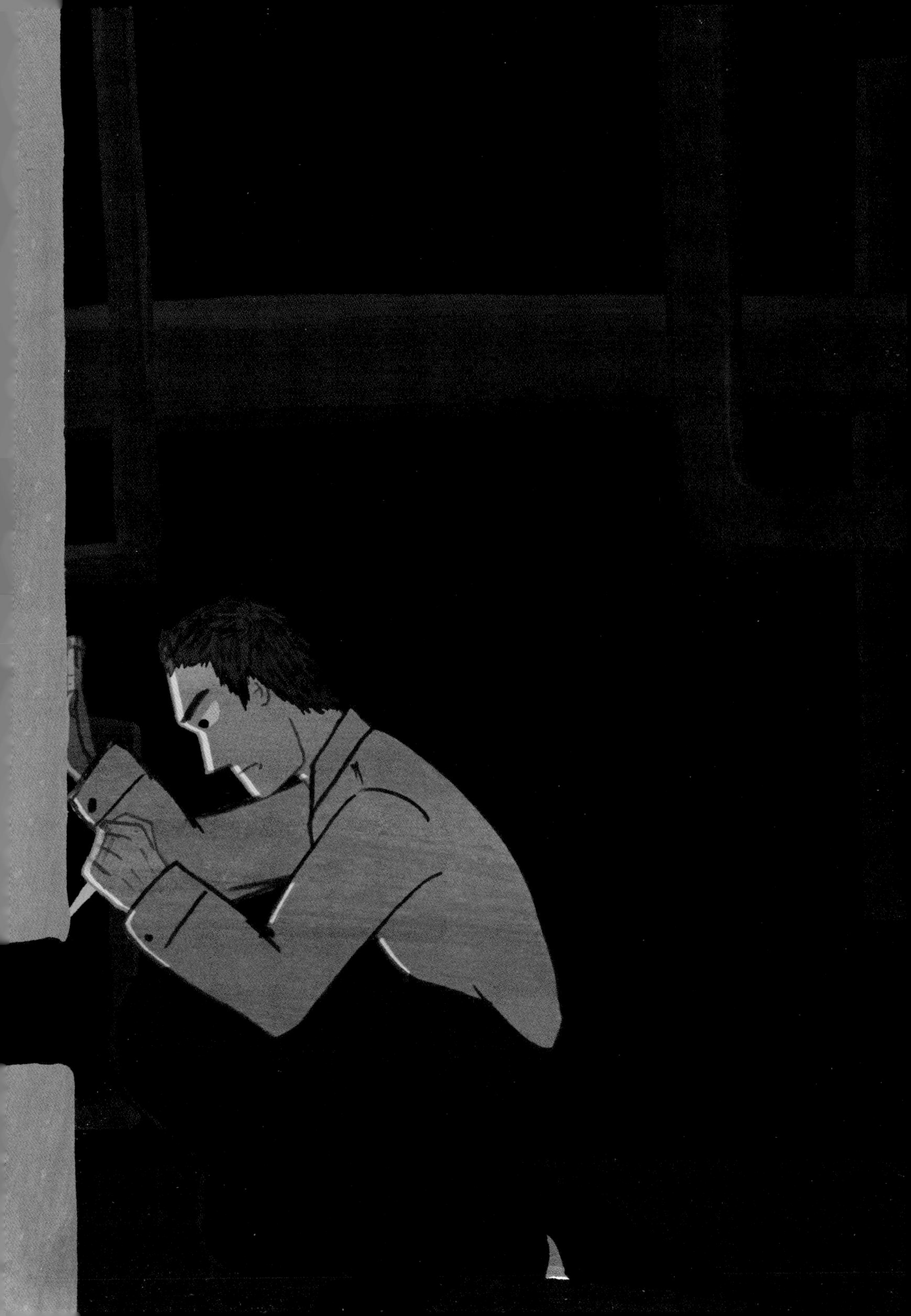

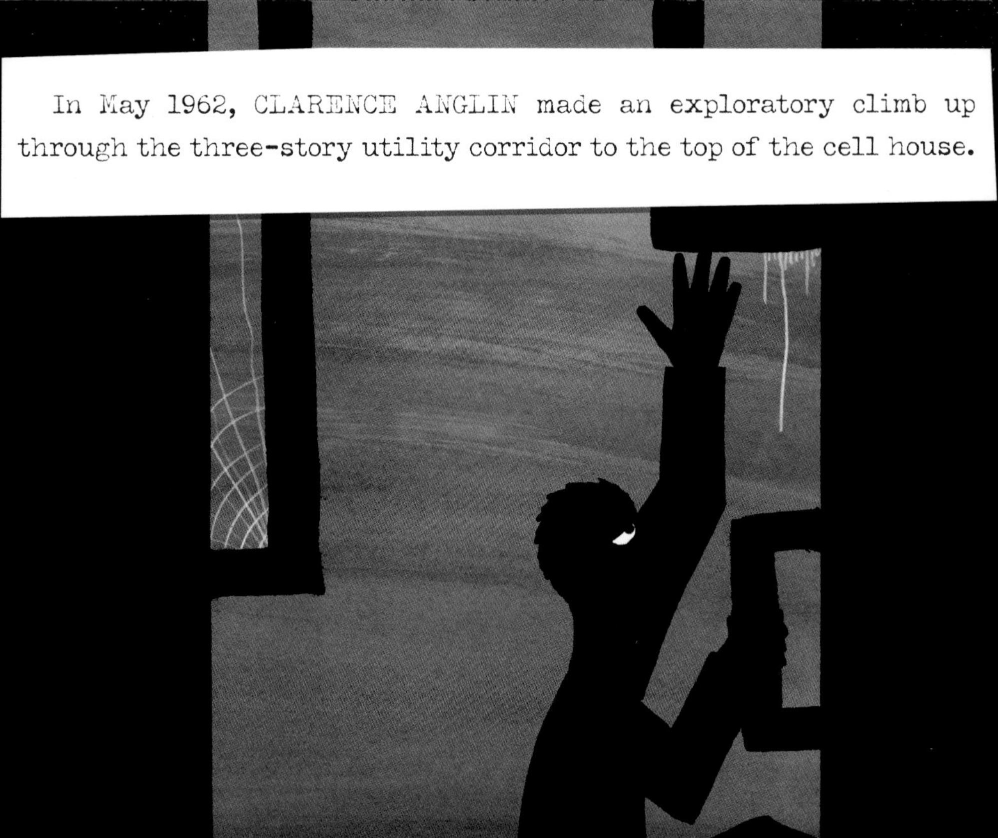
In May 1962, CLARENCE ANGLIN made an exploratory climb up through the three-story utility corridor to the top of the cell house.

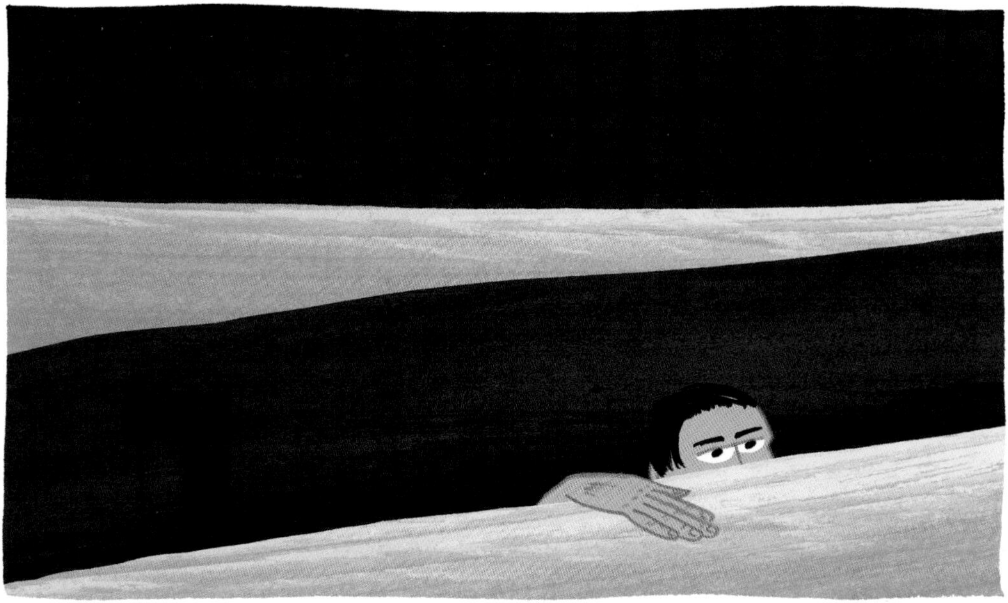

Once there, CLARENCE used a smuggled screwdriver to attempt to pry off the 18½-inch metal grate that covered the roof's ventilator hole, but was unable to make it budge. The men were so close now, but they'd have to figure out another way to get to the roof.

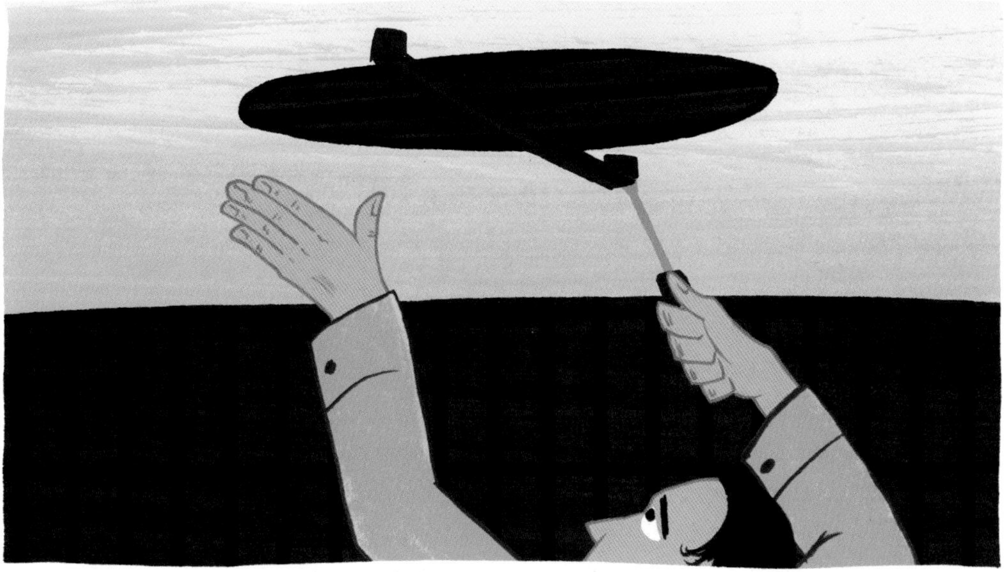

What happened next was either one of the greatest acts of gross negligence by the officials at Alcatraz, or utter ignorance—or a combination of both. Either way, in order to save face, the FBI kept it secret from the public for years to come.

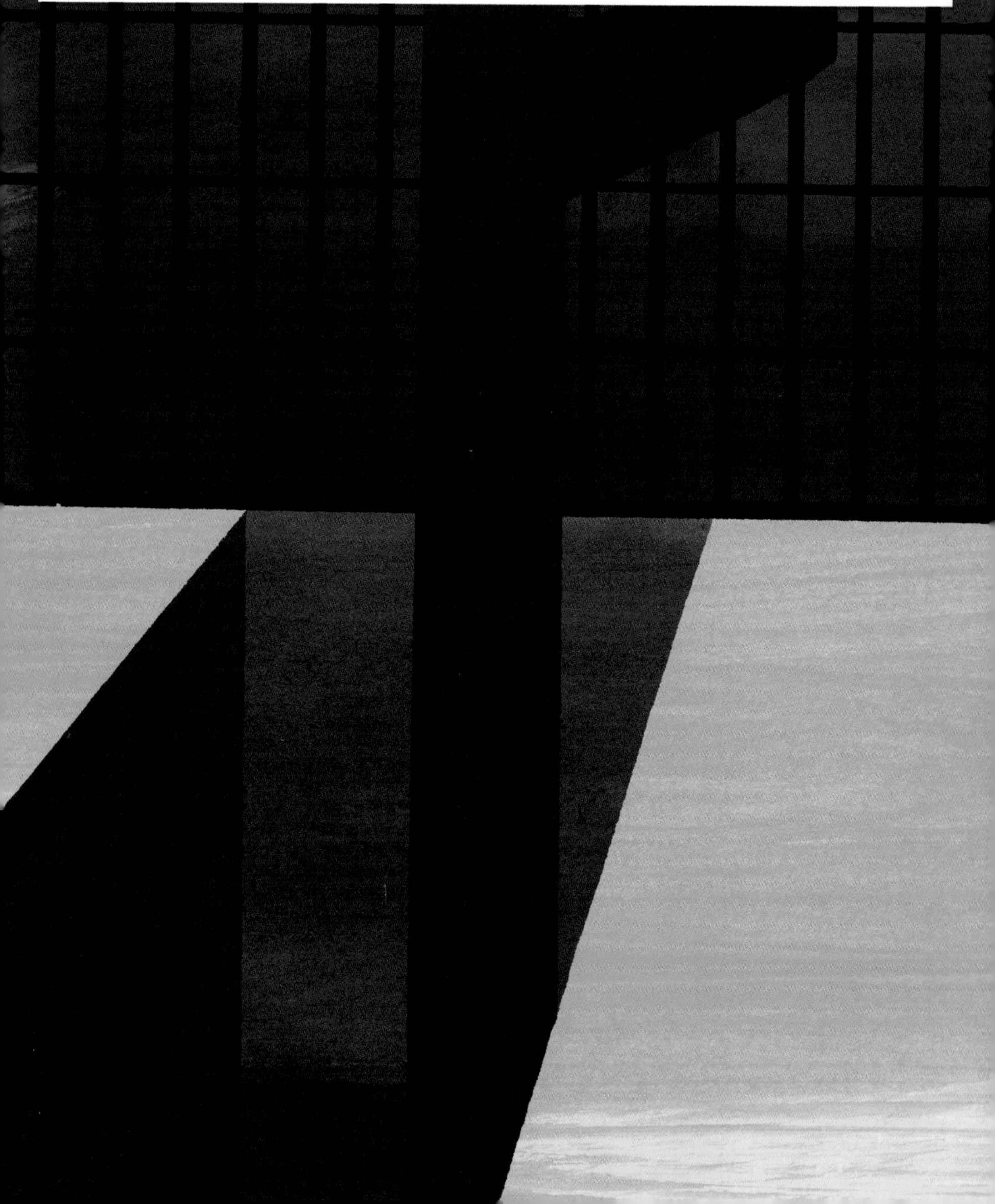

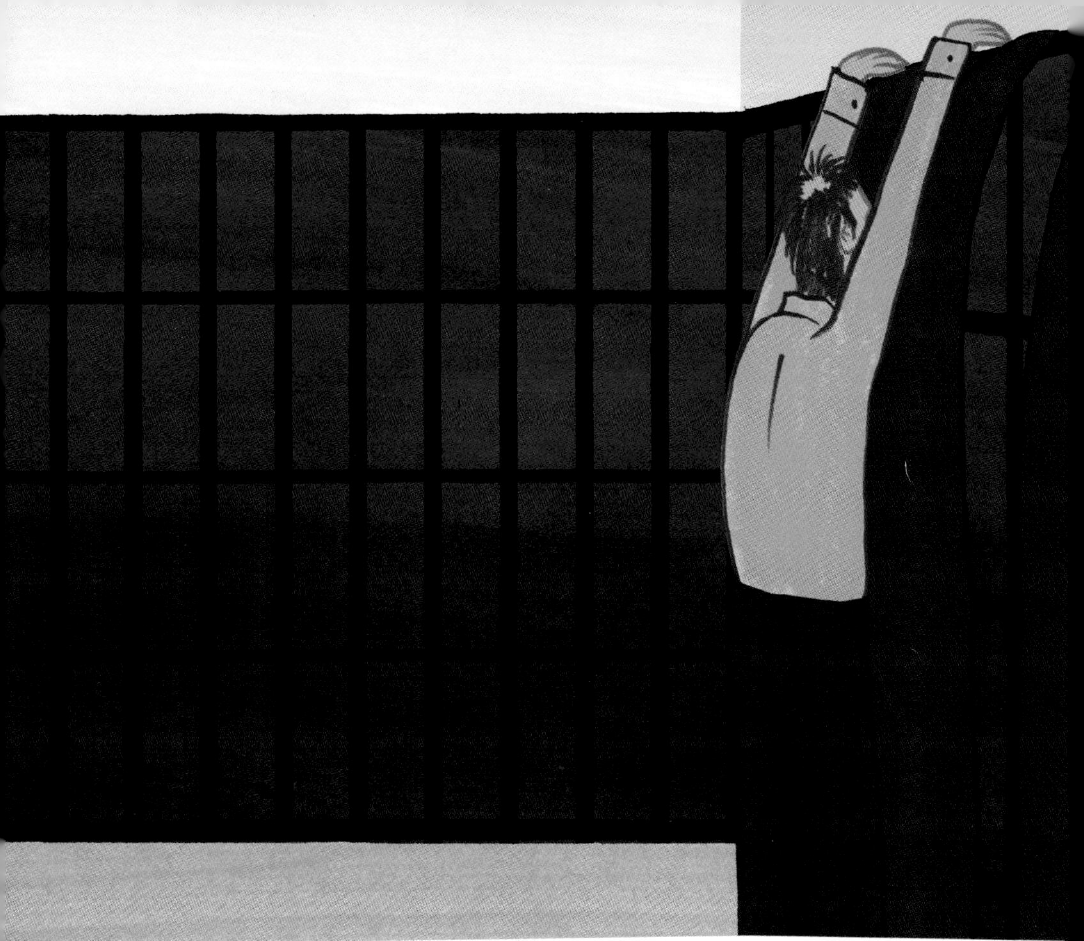

While ALLEN WEST was painting the walls and ceiling in the top area of the cell house, right underneath their escape hatch, he would intentionally make a mess by sweeping dirt and debris over the edge of the catwalk. The dust and the paint chips would fall three stories and land in the cells below. So WEST was permitted to hang blankets from the ceiling in order to contain the mess. This allowed him to create a concealed work area, away from the watchful eyes of the bulls on duty. WEST would paint during the day, and MORRIS and the ANGLINS would sneak up there at night to work on dismantling the security grate that covered the vent's opening, using a homemade wrench. But in order to discreetly get up to the workshop at night without the guards discovering them missing from their beds, the men would need decoys, and that's when CLARENCE ANGLIN came up with an idea.

With the same papier-mâché recipe that he had used on the replacement vents, CLARENCE created a dummy head that he affectionately referred to as "Oink." He painstakingly sculpted it from rags, and then layered soap, shredded magazine pages, concrete dust, and a glue mixture on top of it. He was also able to order paint that matched their skin color directly from the prison's commissary to make the dummy more lifelike. CLARENCE even painted some portraits in his cell, so that no one would wonder why he had ordered that particular color.

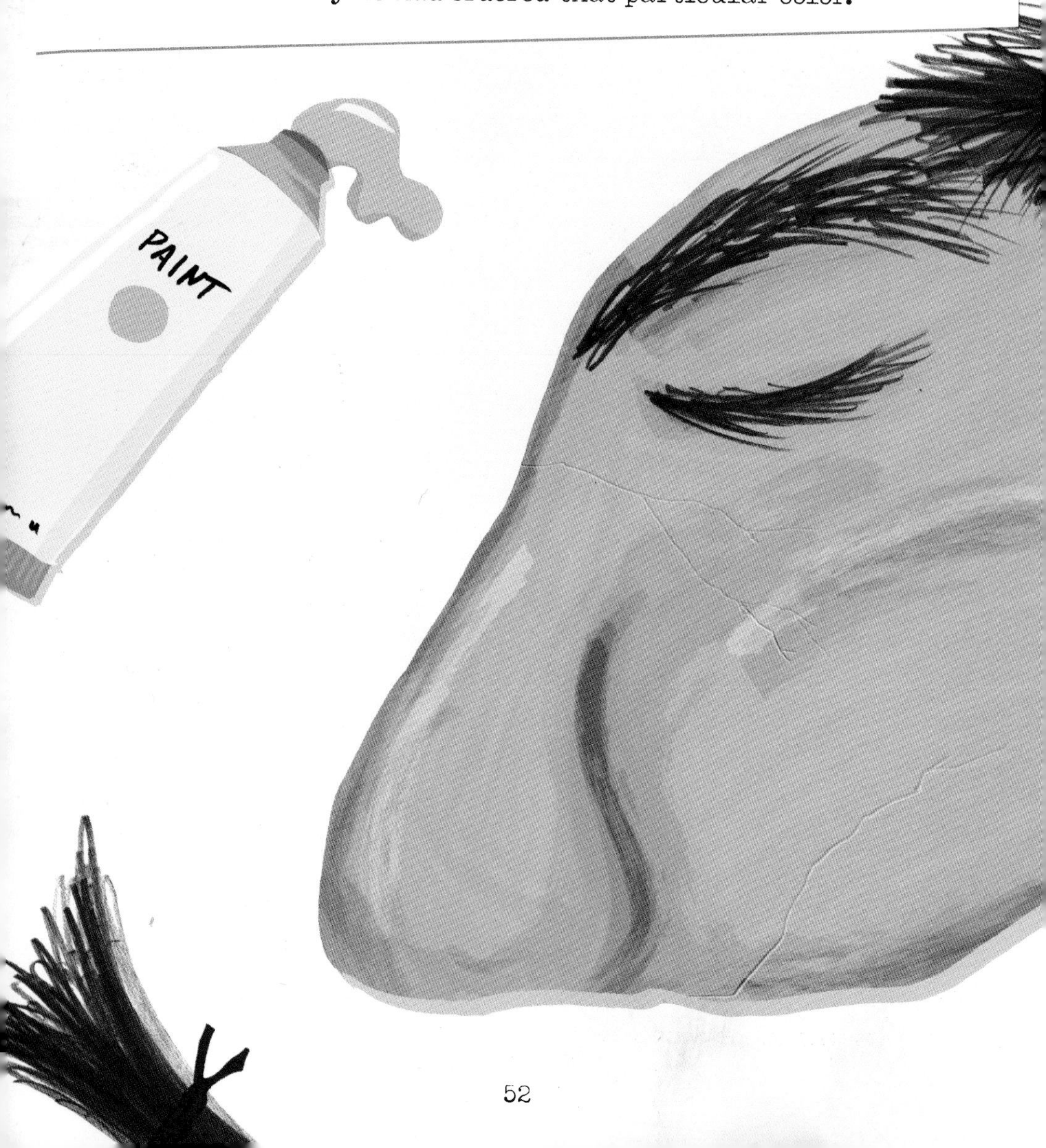
PAINT

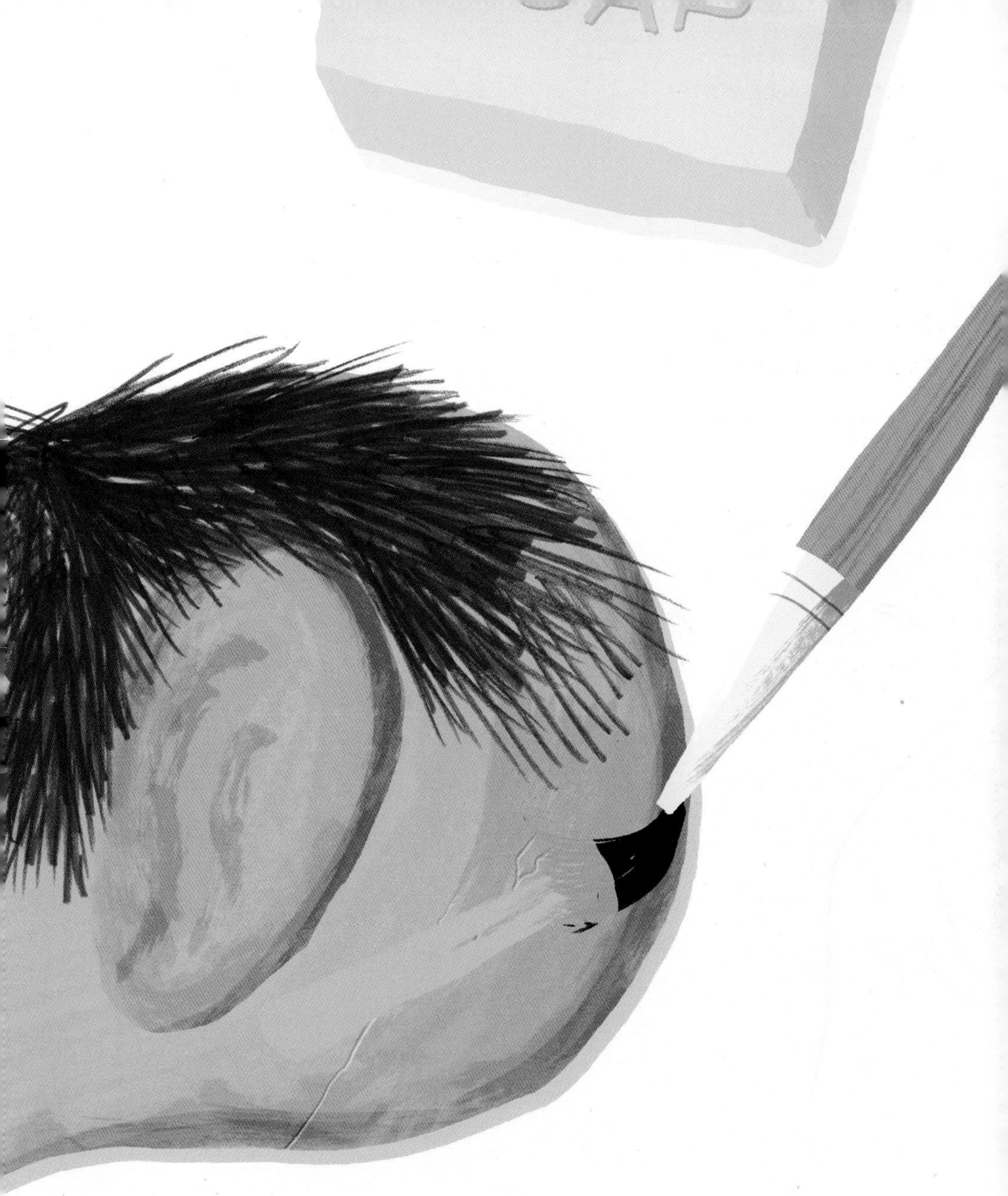

To make the dummy head more realistic, CLARENCE—who worked a detail in the prison's barbershop—collected human hair clippings for his project. "Oink" would serve as a prototype for the heads he would create for the other convicts.

The final obstacle was the mile and a quarter swim across the 50-degree water of the San Francisco Bay, and once again, the prison magazine library came in handy.

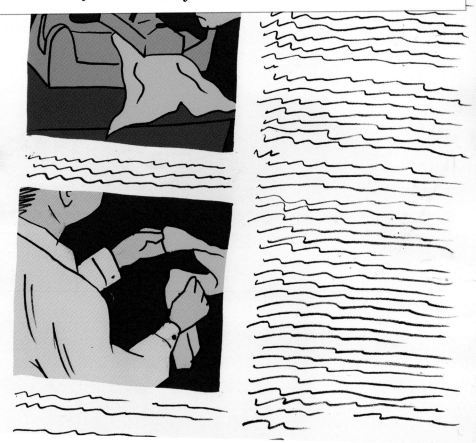

The November 1960 issue of *Popular Mechanics* contained an article about a goose hunter named J.C. SCHULTZ, who determined that an inflatable rubber goose decoy would be better than the clunky wooden ones on the market. The article detailed how SCHULTZ created a pattern that he cut out of rubber inner tubes, then how he sealed the rubber seams using vulcanization, which is a method of hardening rubber by treating it with heat. The article even described how to insert a valve to inflate the rubber goose. JOHN ANGLIN was able to apply these techniques to make an inflatable raft from over fifty raincoats that the men had stolen or acquired from other inmates.

The March 1962 issue of *Popular Mechanics* contained an article about life preservers, which JOHN ANGLIN also designed for the men out of raincoats. FRANK MORRIS had a copy of the May 21, 1962, issue of *Sports Illustrated*, which included information about docking and undocking boats, as well as a guide to buoys, water safety symbols, and tips for navigating busy waterways.

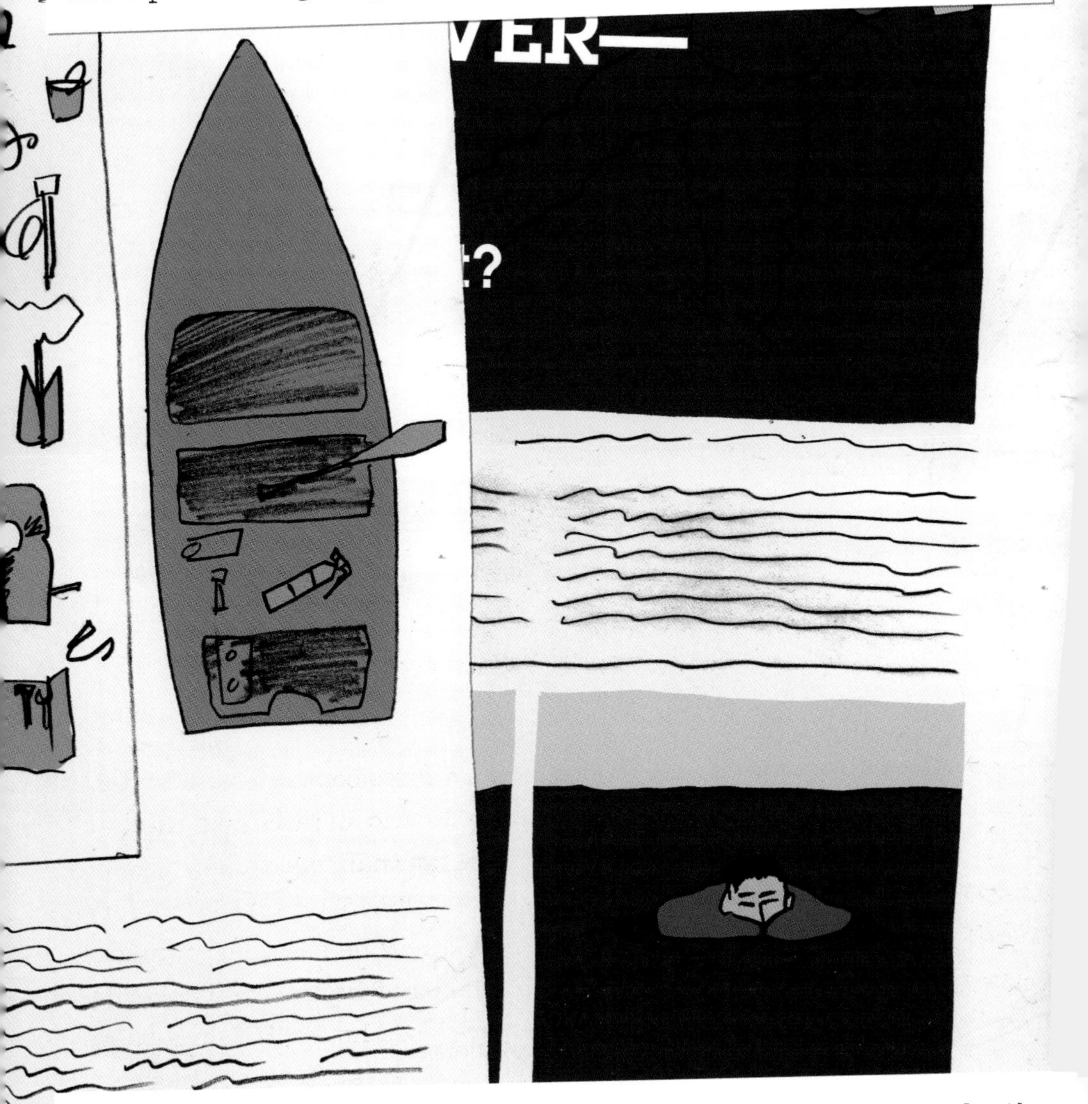

After months of hard work, the time had finally come to make the escape.

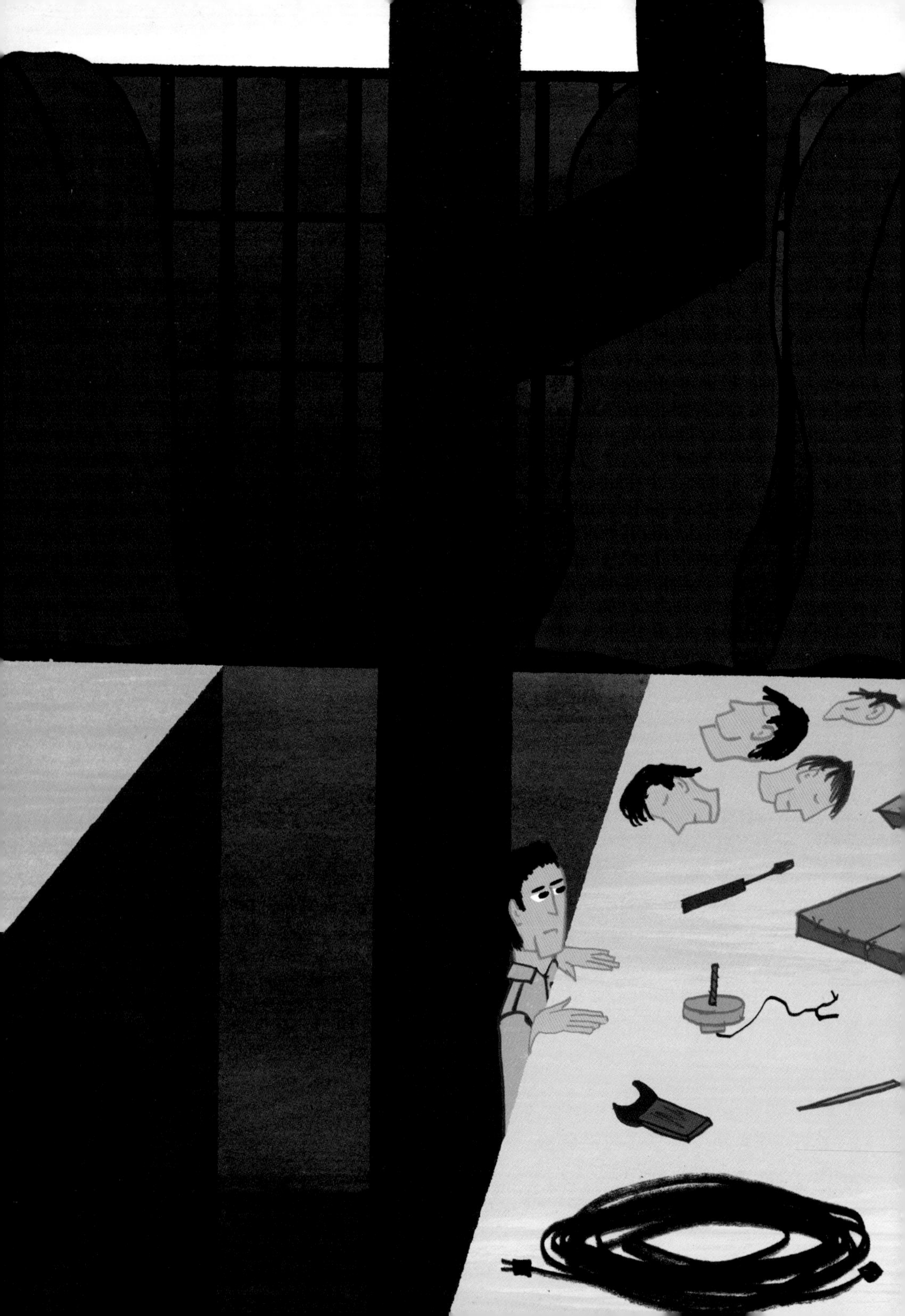

# PART SIX:
# THE ESCAPE

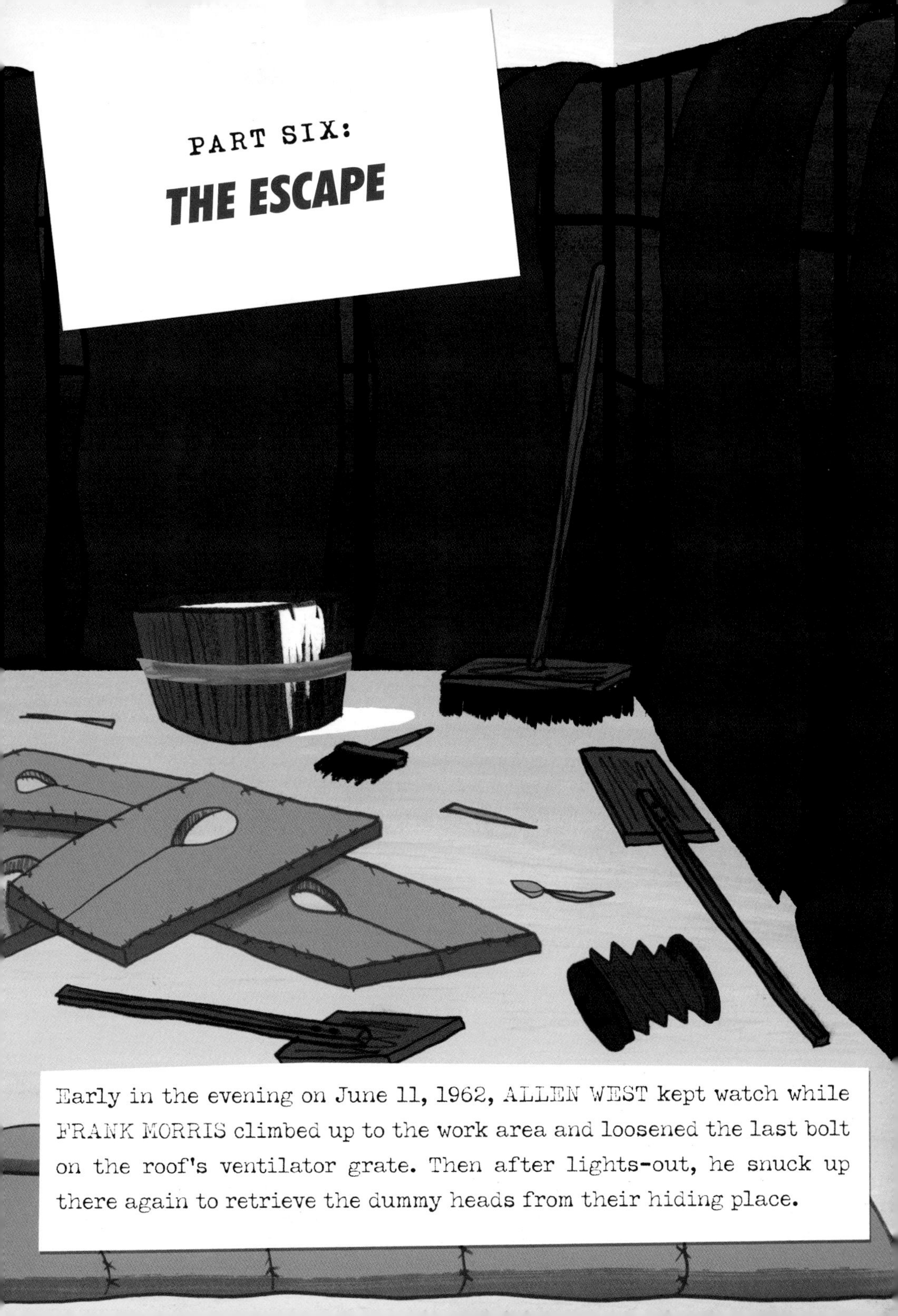
Early in the evening on June 11, 1962, ALLEN WEST kept watch while FRANK MORRIS climbed up to the work area and loosened the last bolt on the roof's ventilator grate. Then after lights-out, he snuck up there again to retrieve the dummy heads from their hiding place.

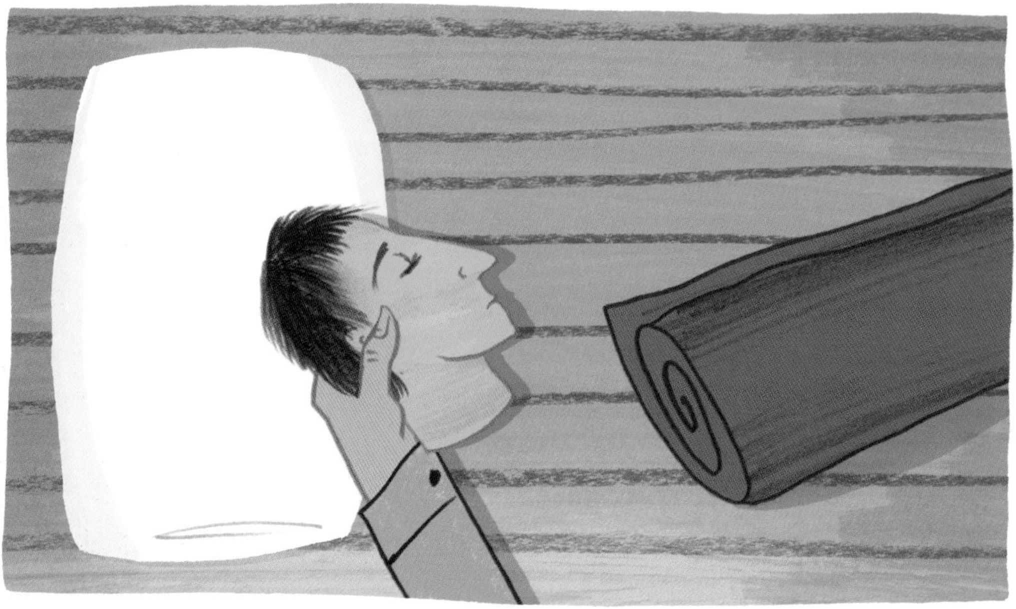

The men stuffed jackets and extra blankets under the covers on their beds, placed the dummy heads on their pillows, and then climbed through the ventilator holes and into the utility corridor. But ALLEN WEST was nowhere to be seen.

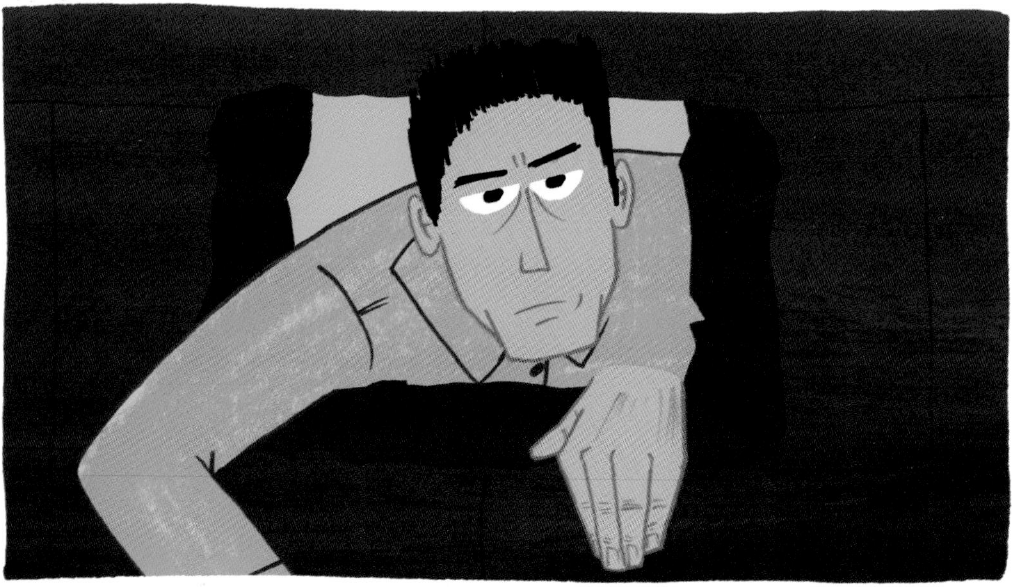

As it turned out, WEST had never fully finished digging out his vent. His primary job had been to construct life jackets and wooden paddles, as well as to keep watch, but he had never actually set foot in the corridor. CLARENCE ANGLIN tried to dig out WEST'S vent from the back, and even gave the concrete a few good kicks. But time was short, and if they were too loud, the guards might hear them. So the men had no choice but to leave WEST behind.

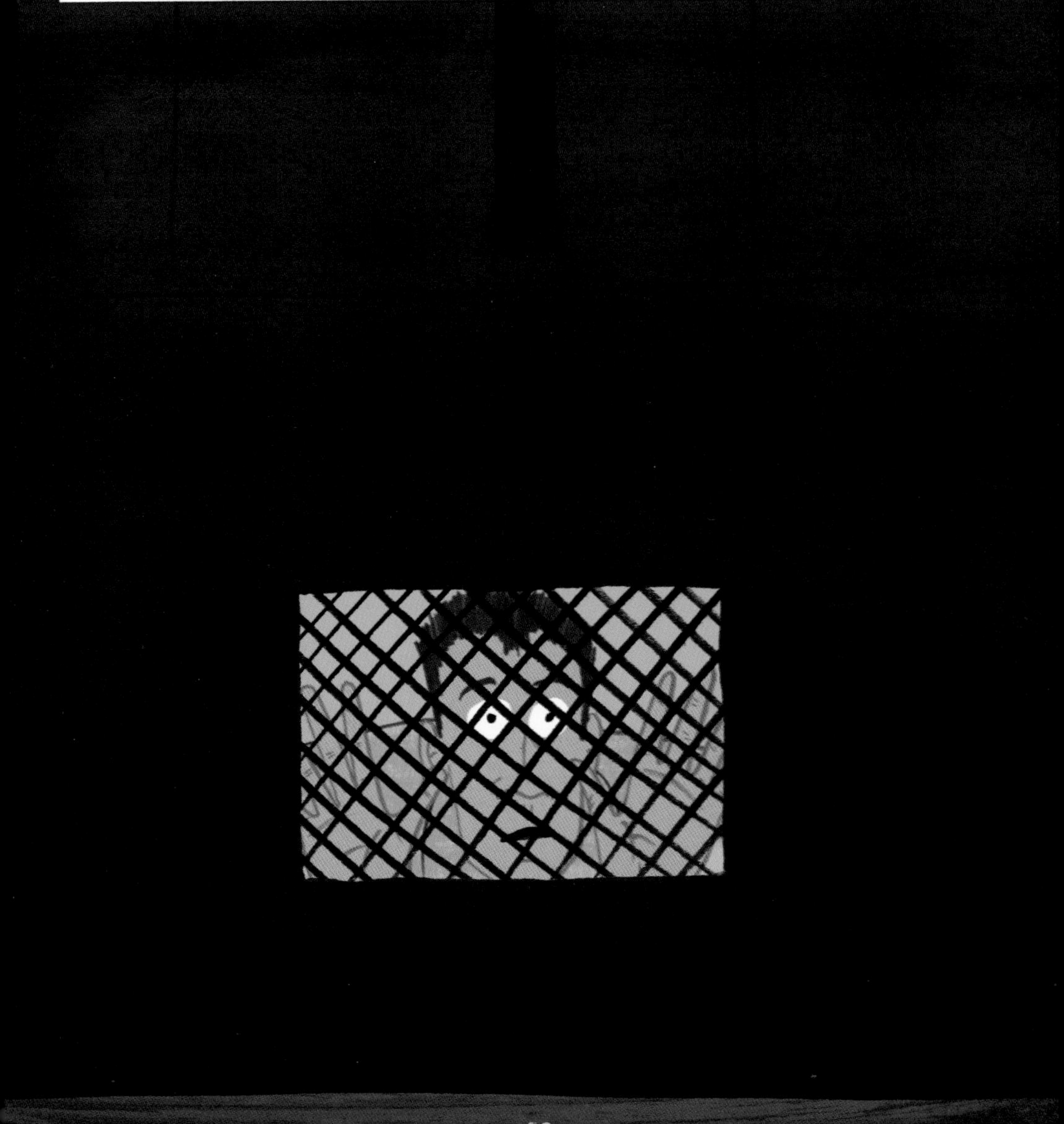

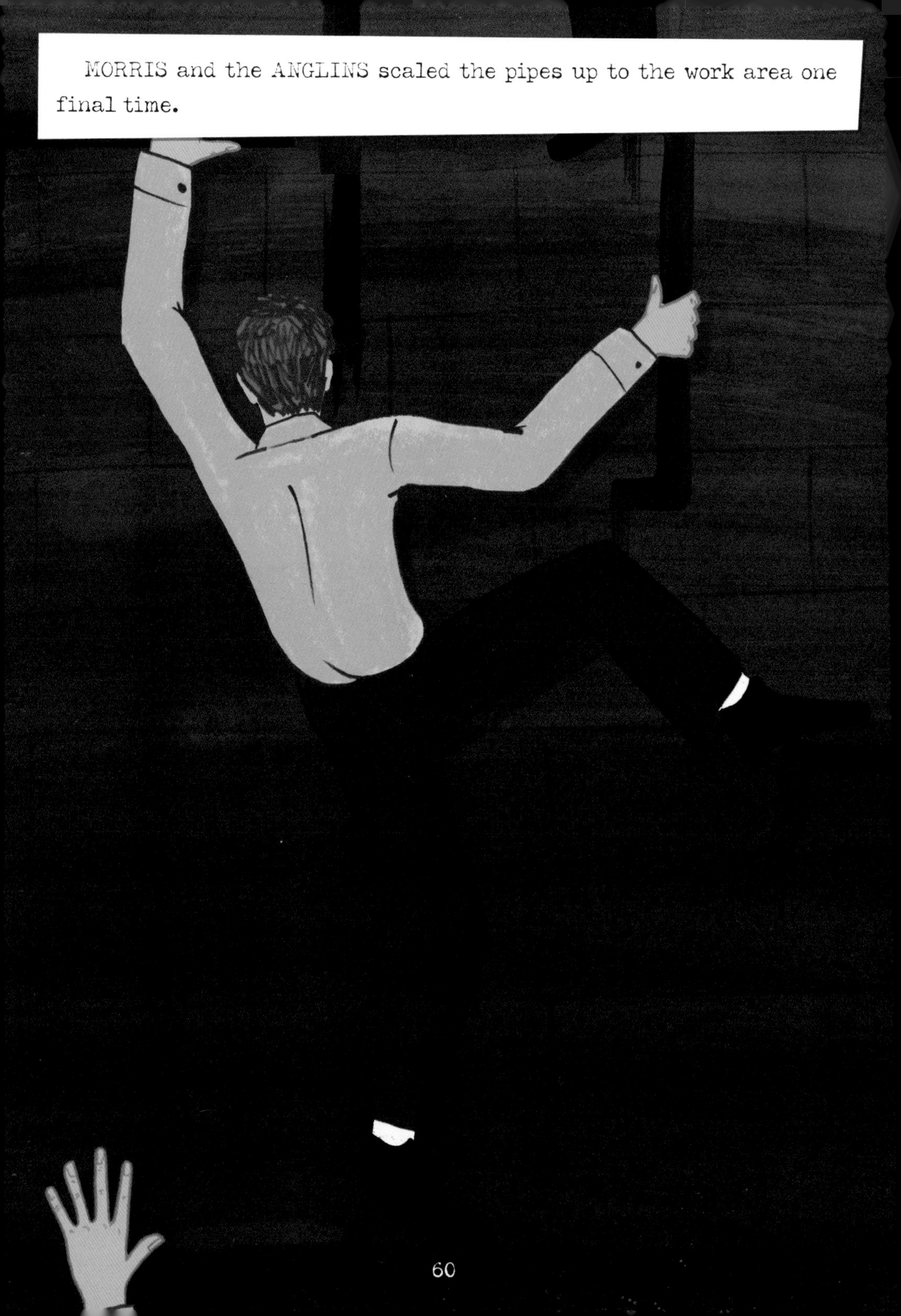
MORRIS and the ANGLINS scaled the pipes up to the work area one final time.

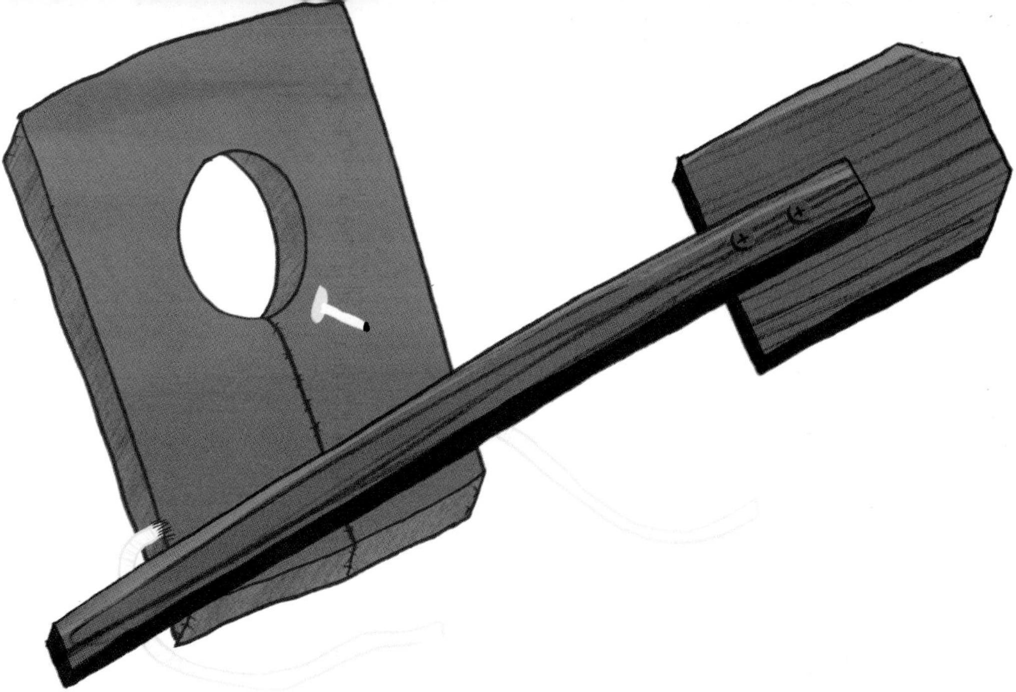

They knew there was a chance that WEST might eventually make it out of his cell, so they left behind a paddle, a life jacket, and an uninflated raft. The inmates then removed the bolts from the vent covering and pushed it up through the shaft.

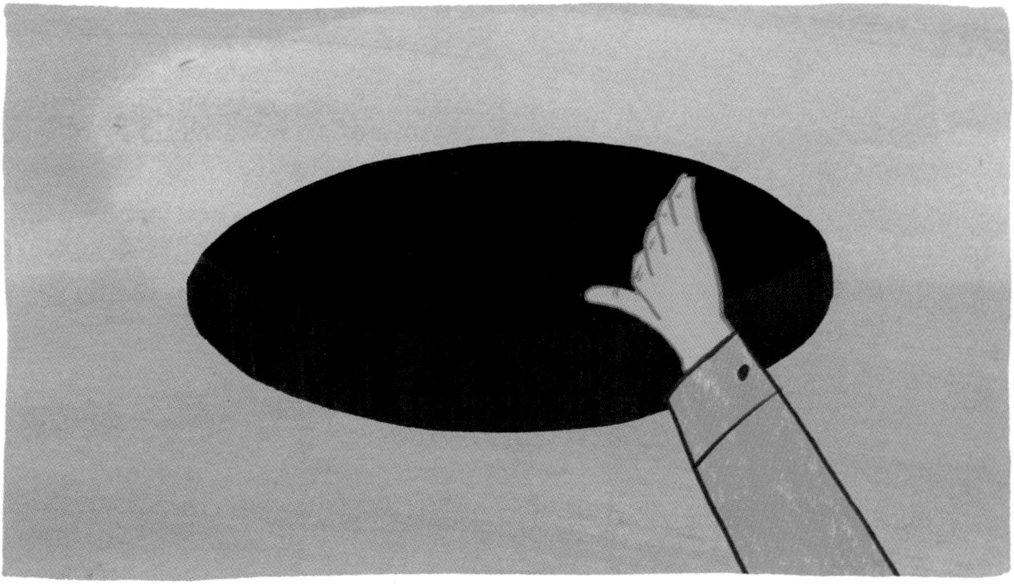

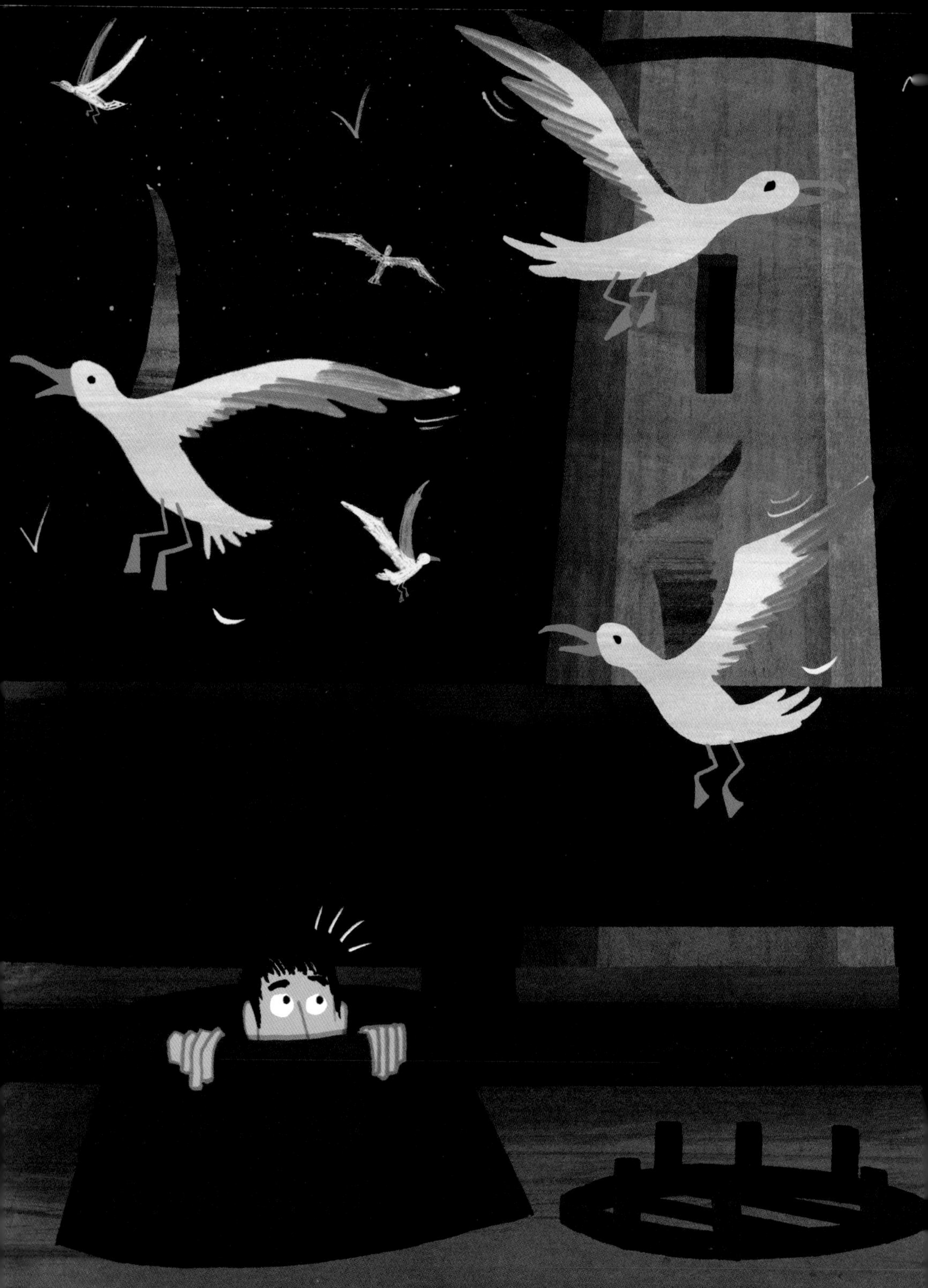

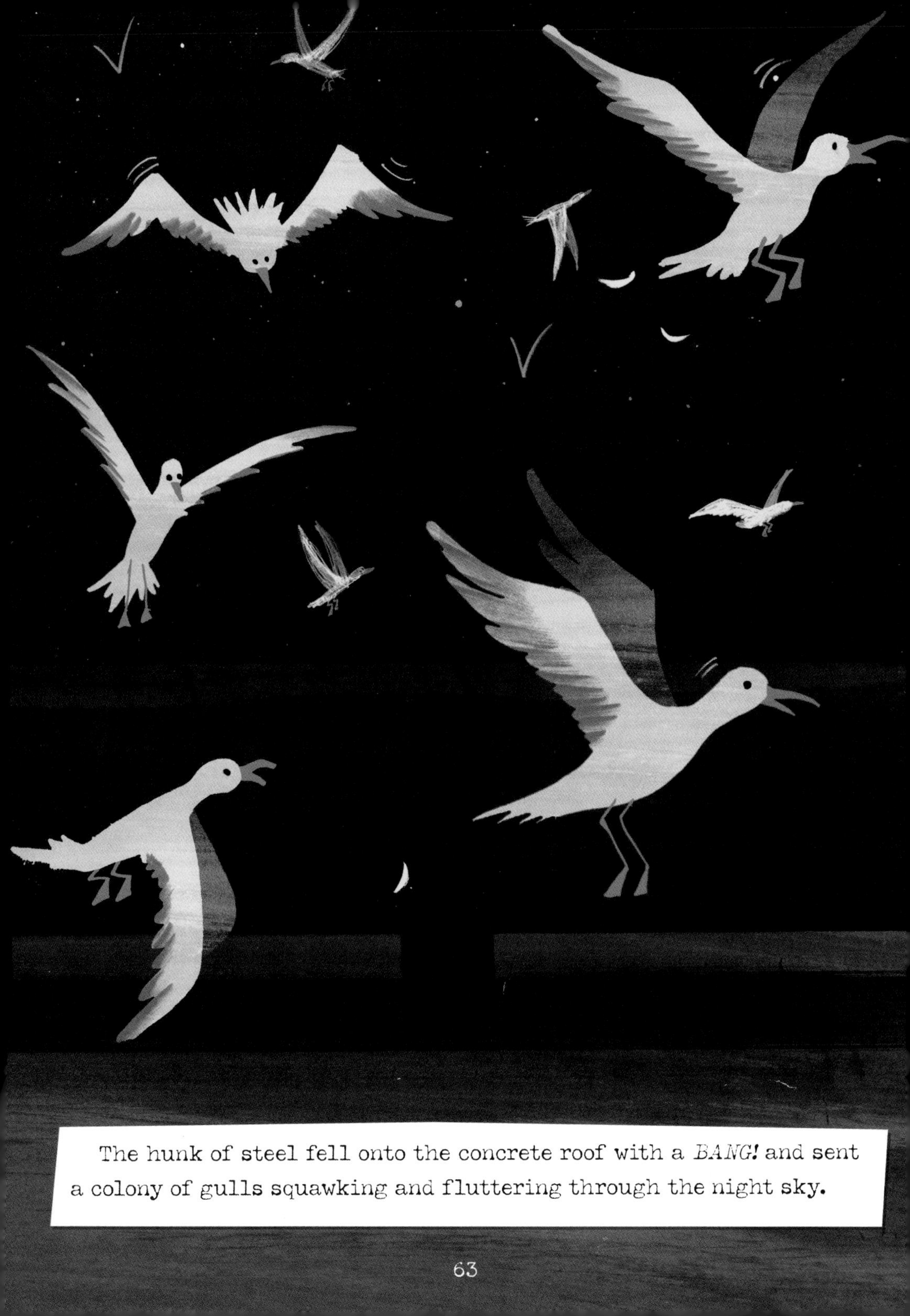

The hunk of steel fell onto the concrete roof with a *BANG!* and sent a colony of gulls squawking and fluttering through the night sky.

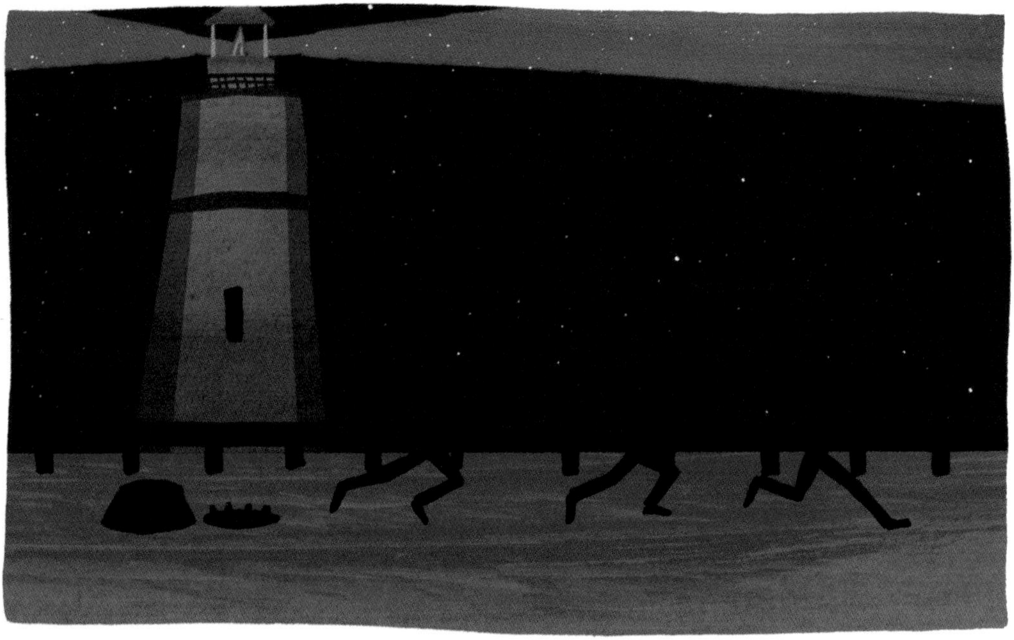

MORRIS and the ANGLIN brothers scuttled across the roof and descended the 50-foot duct pipe to the ground below.

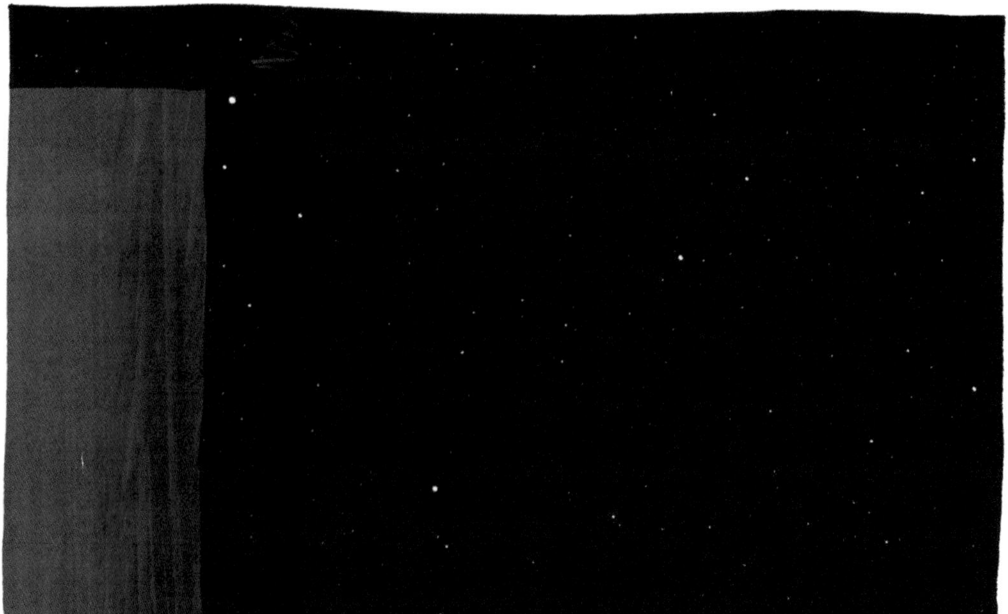

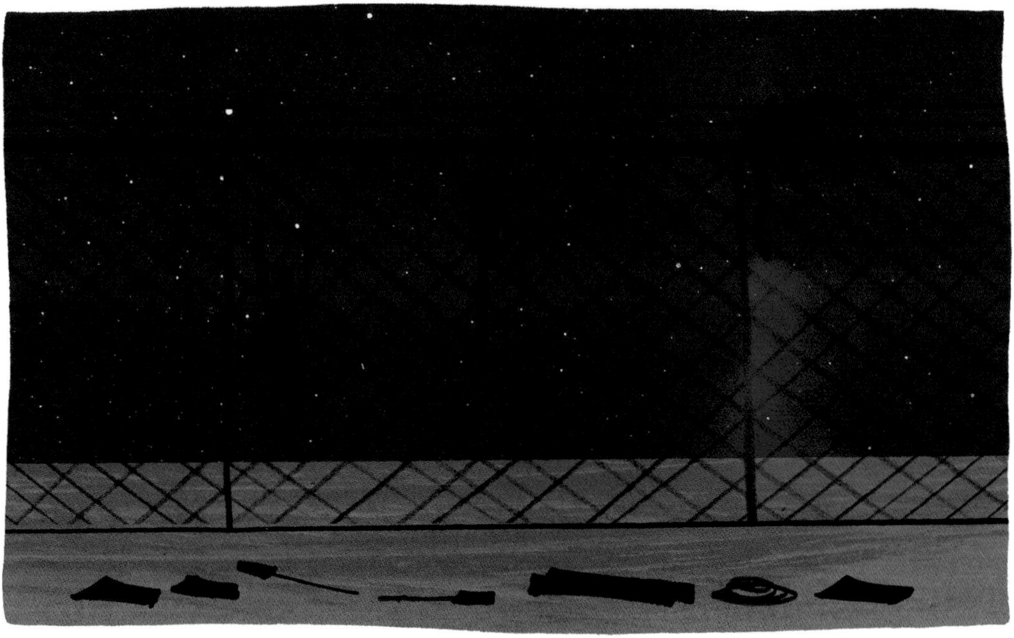

They then scaled two separate fences and made their way to the water's edge.

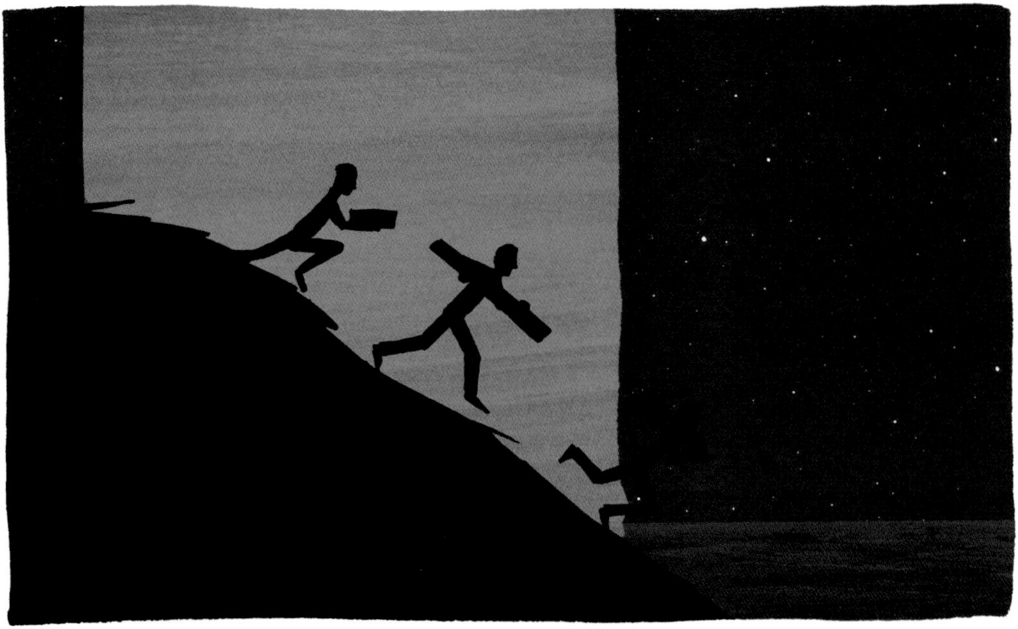

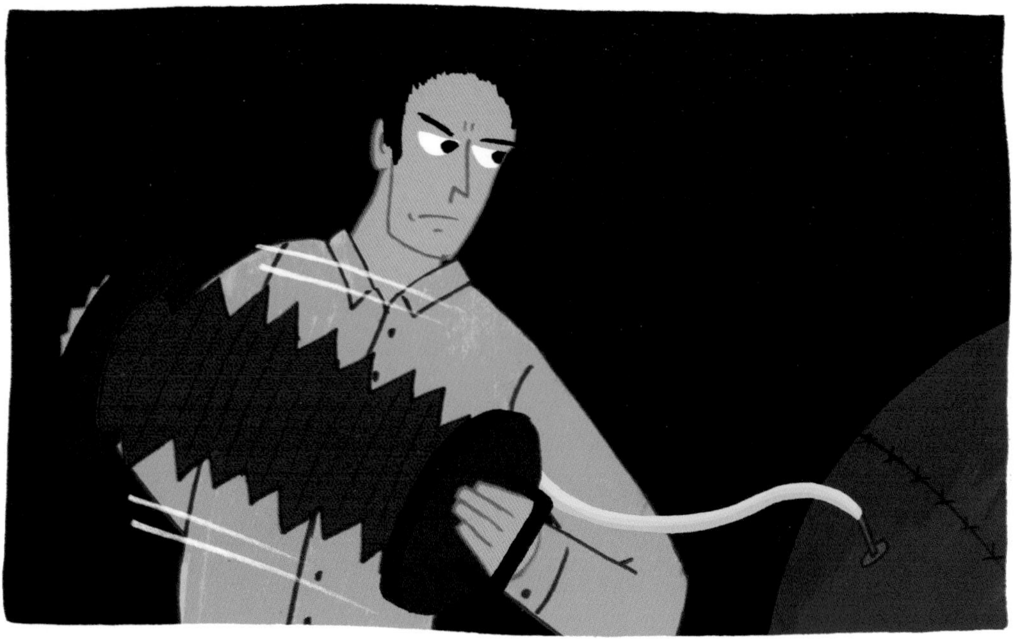

They inflated the makeshift raft using a concertina, a type of accordion, that FRANK MORRIS had modified from a noisy instrument into a silent air pump.

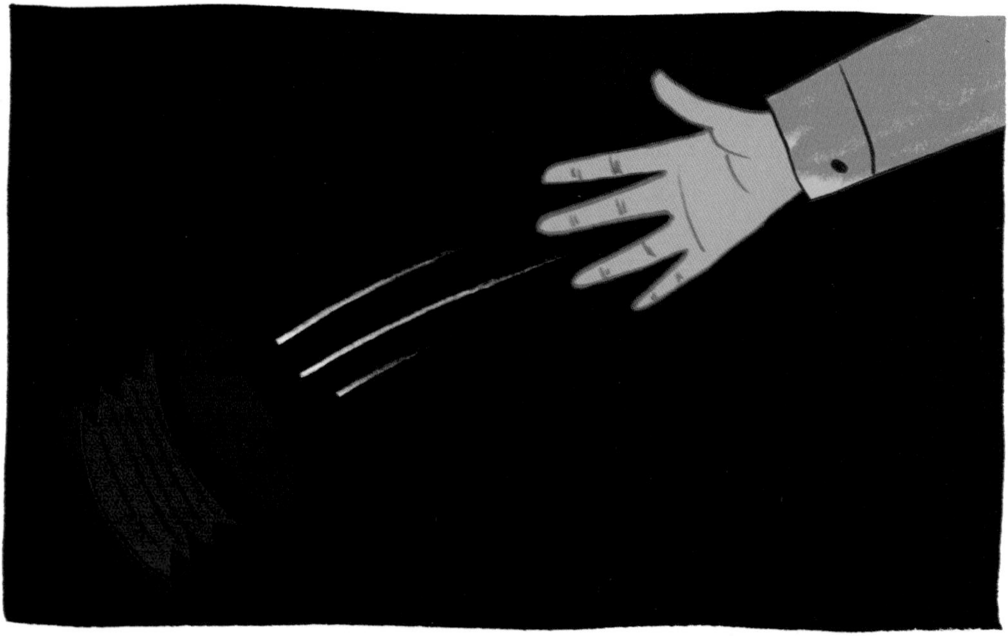

The men then discarded any unneeded items and pushed off into the water.

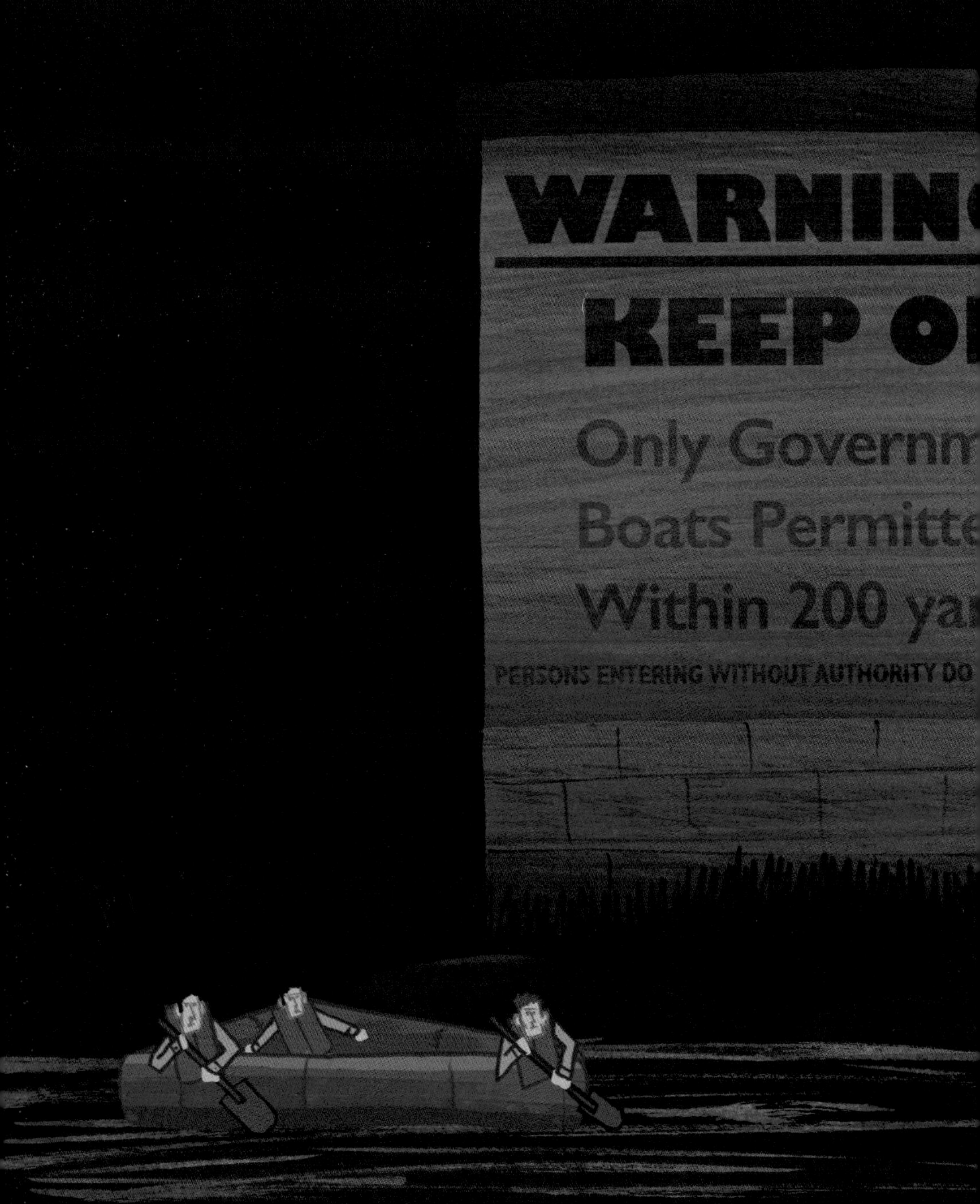
WARNIN
KEEP O
Only Governm
Boats Permitte
Within 200 ya
PERSONS ENTERING WITHOUT AUTHORITY DO

They paddled out into the bay . . .

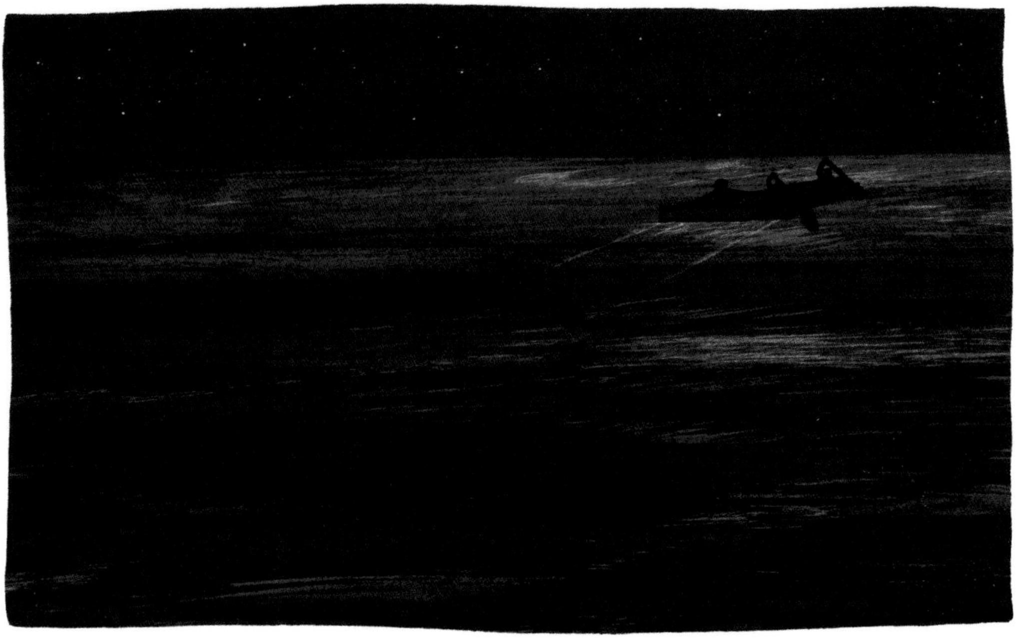

... and disappeared under the cover of darkness ...

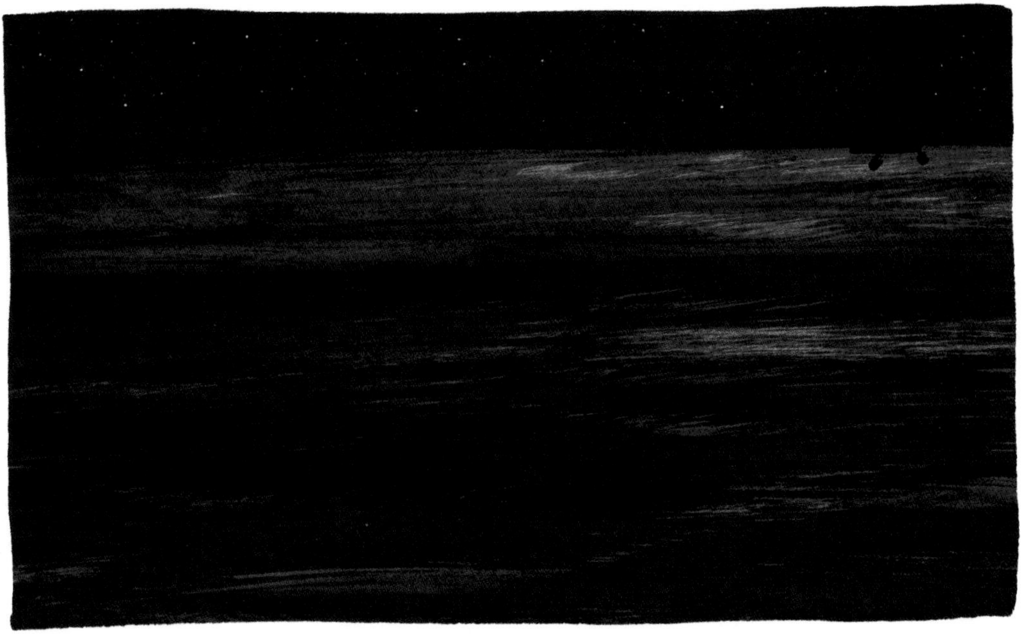

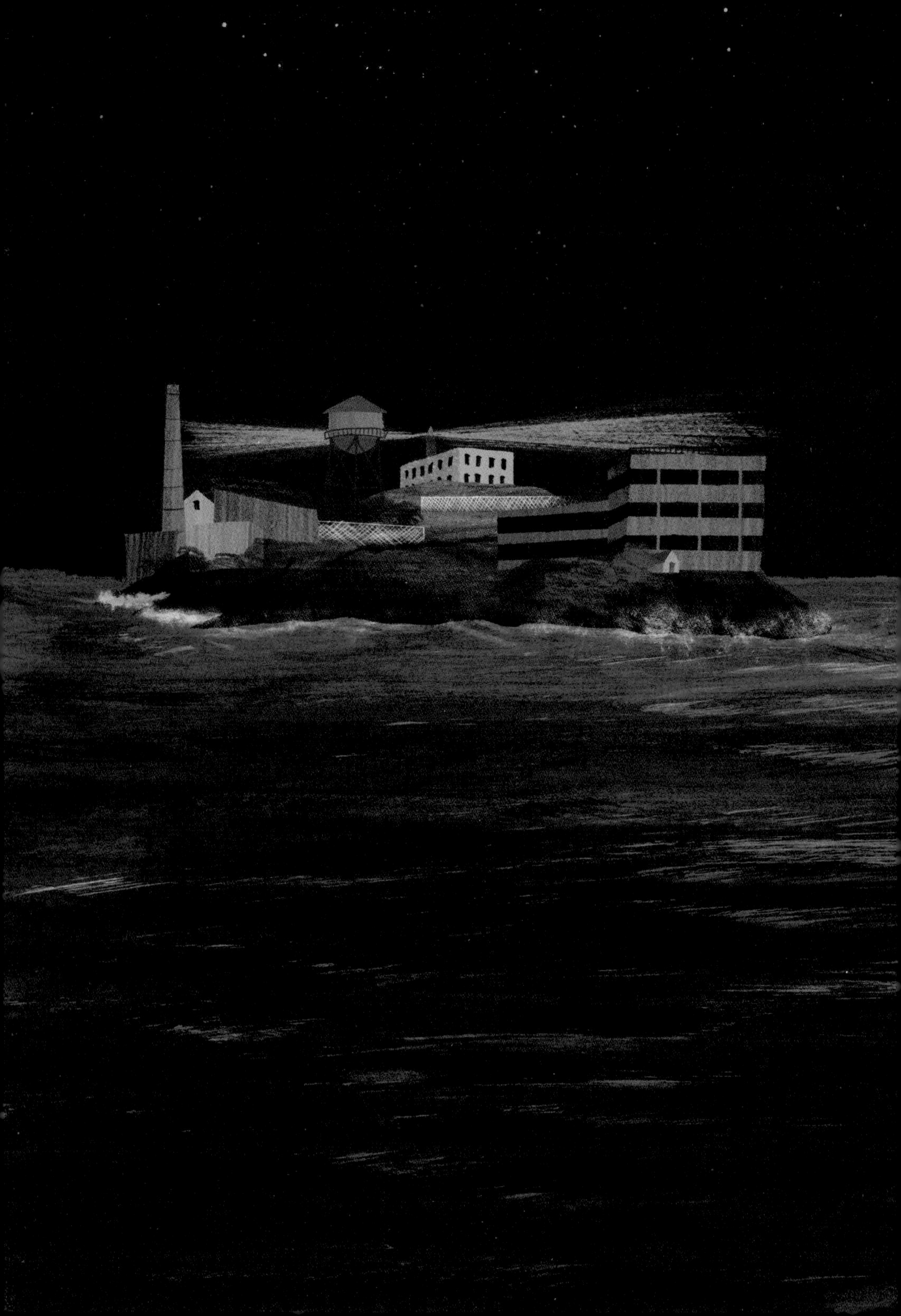

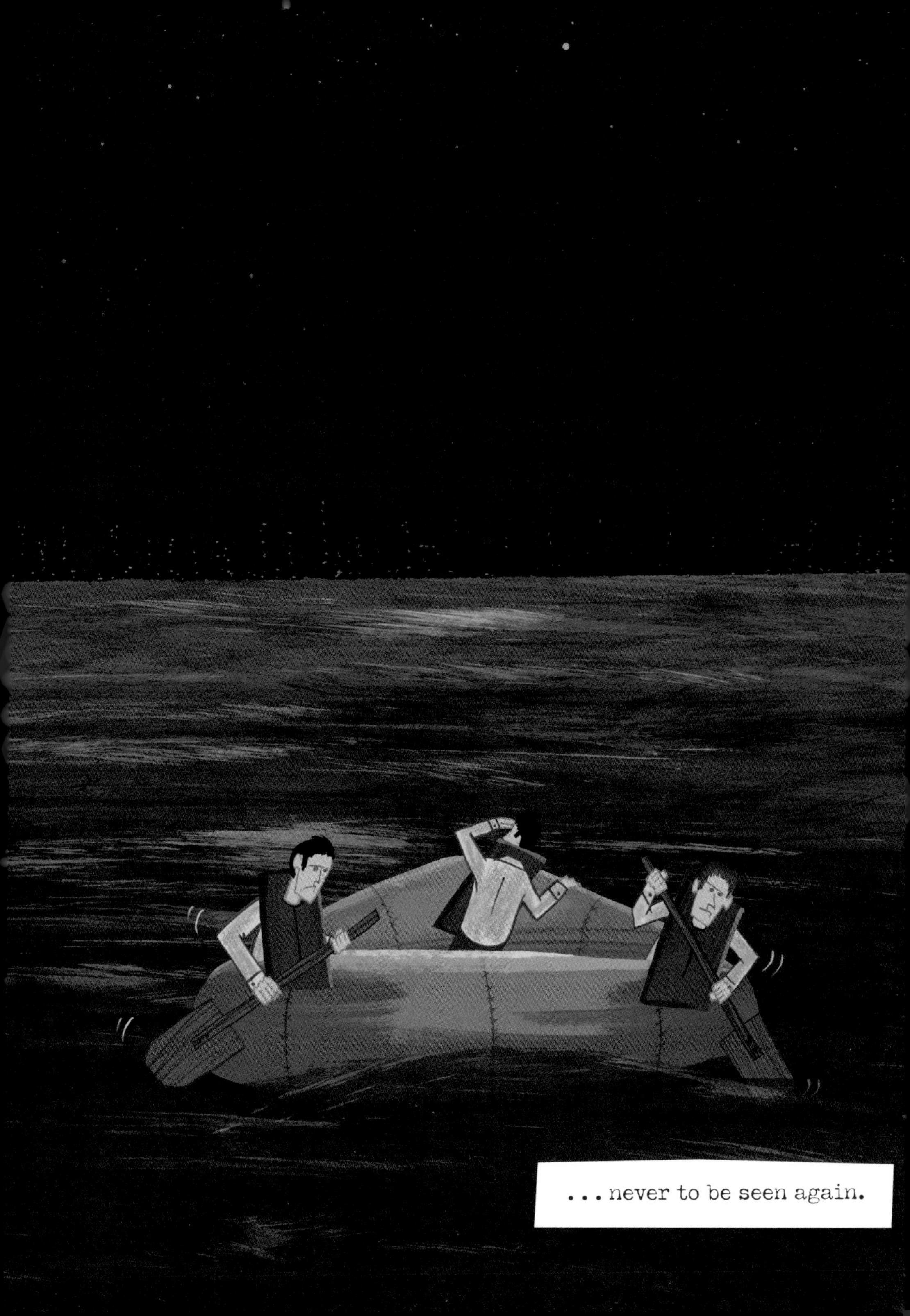
. . . never to be seen again.

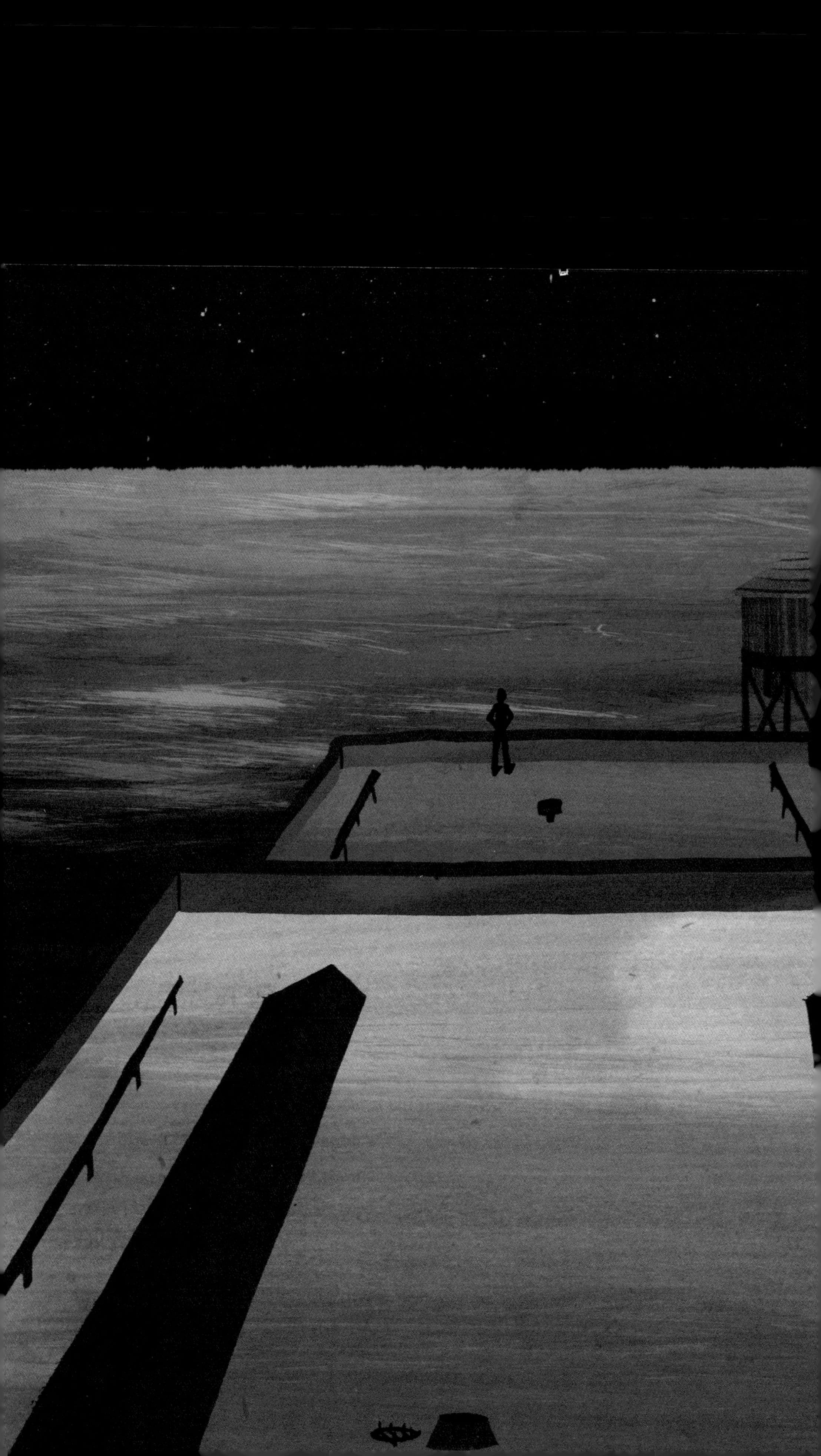

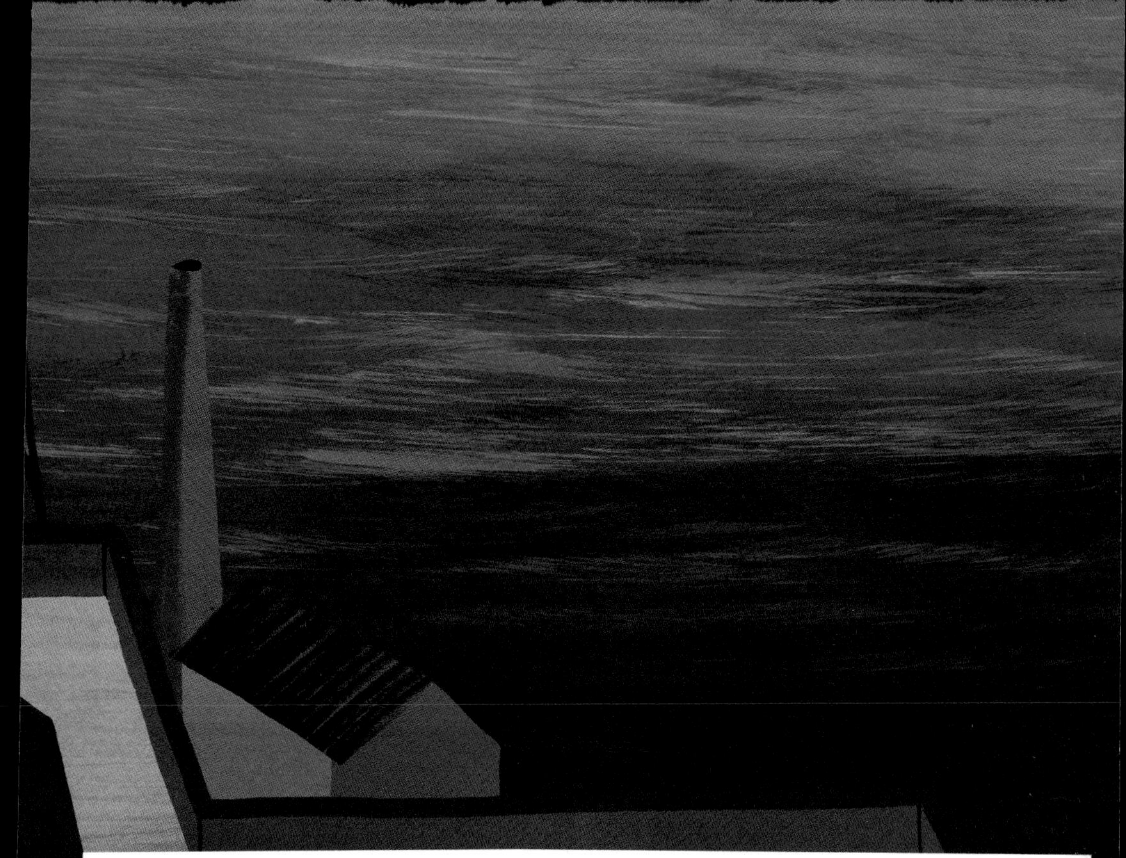

Meanwhile, it was almost two in the morning by the time ALLEN WEST finally breached his cell wall. He raced up the pipes to the work area, but he was too late, and the others were already long gone. Perhaps he weighed his options and didn't like the odds of making it alone. Or perhaps he was a history student when it came to previous escape attempts, and he figured that MORRIS and the ANGLINS were most likely fish food by now. Either way, he hung around for a couple of hours before giving up and snaking his way back down to his cell just before dawn.

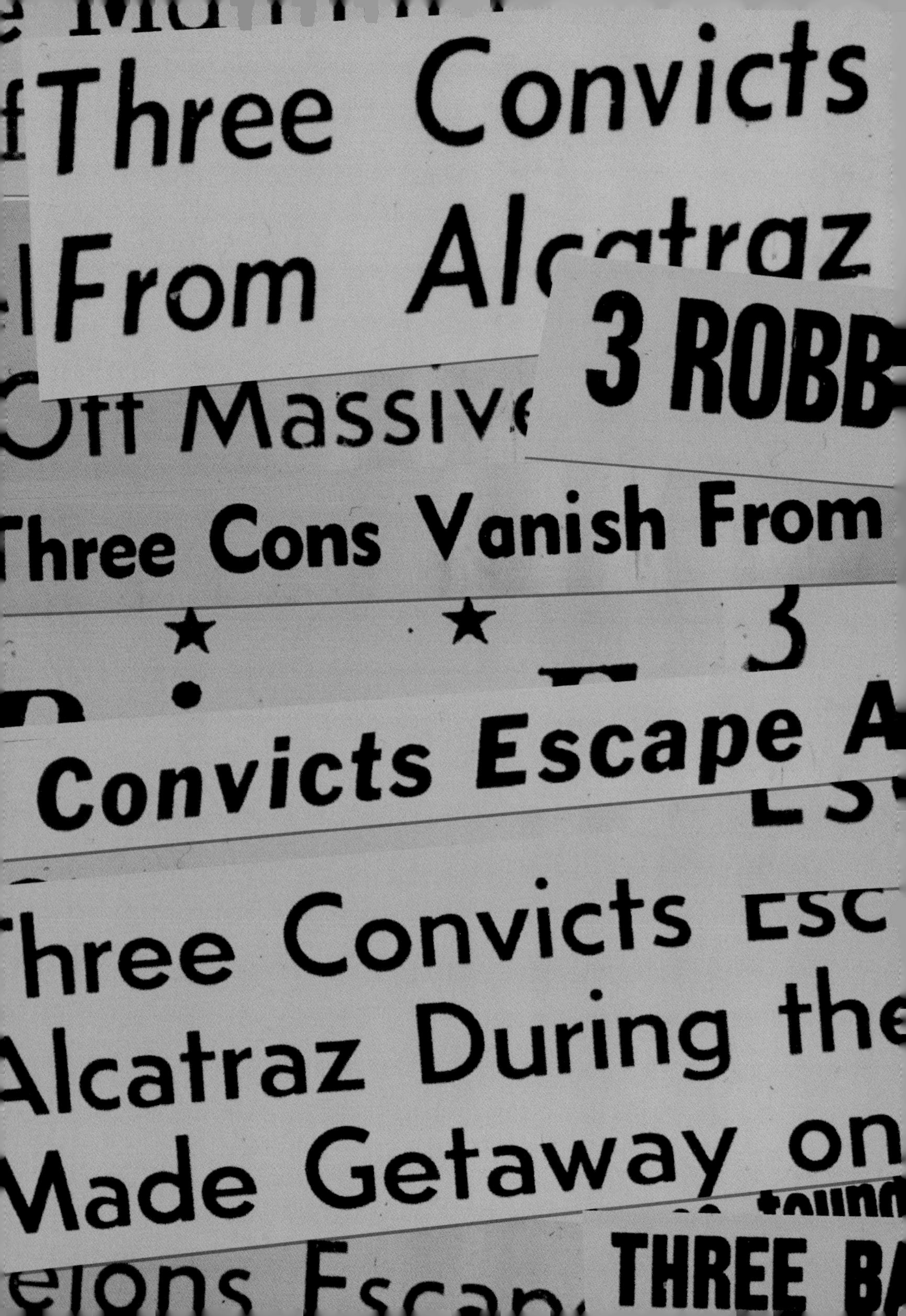

Three Convicts
From Alcatraz
3 ROBB
Off Massiv
Three Cons Vanish From
Convicts Escape A
Three Convicts Esc
Alcatraz During the
Made Getaway on
THREE BA

scape

Prison

S ESCAPE ALCATRAZ

ank Robbers

atraz Alcatraz

DUMMIES LEFT IN BUNKS

Search Widens

Once the guards realized the men were missing, the FBI was notified, and they launched their largest manhunt in over thirty years. They searched air, land, and sea—fruitlessly. To everyone's shock, three dangerous men had pulled off the impossible, and had somehow managed to actually escape from Alcatraz.

ROBBERS FLEE ALCATRA

Federal agents interrogated ALLEN WEST, who was the only source of firsthand knowledge about the escape. They knew not to completely trust everything a convict told them, but between his testimony and the evidence left behind, they were able to deduce the rest of the inmates' scheme.

The men had planned to paddle to nearby ANGEL ISLAND, where they would slash and sink the raft and life jackets in order to destroy the evidence of their route. They would then make their way over to the west side of the island before swimming across RACCOON STRAIT and on to MARIN COUNTY. Once there, the plan was to steal a car, break into a department store to steal clothes, and then drive to MEXICO.

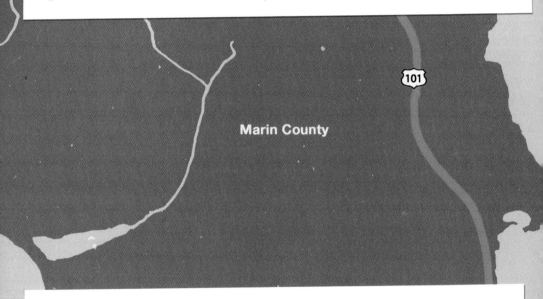

Marin County

101

In line with ALLEN WEST'S testimony, a 1955 blue Chevy was reported stolen in Marin County on the day after the escape. A man reported to the California Highway Patrol that he had been forced off the road by three men in a blue Chevrolet who matched the suspects' descriptions. But the vehicle and its occupants were never discovered.

Interestingly enough, the details surrounding the Chevy's theft were not made public until well after the fact, so the tipster would not have had any idea that the three mysterious men were in any way connected to the escape.

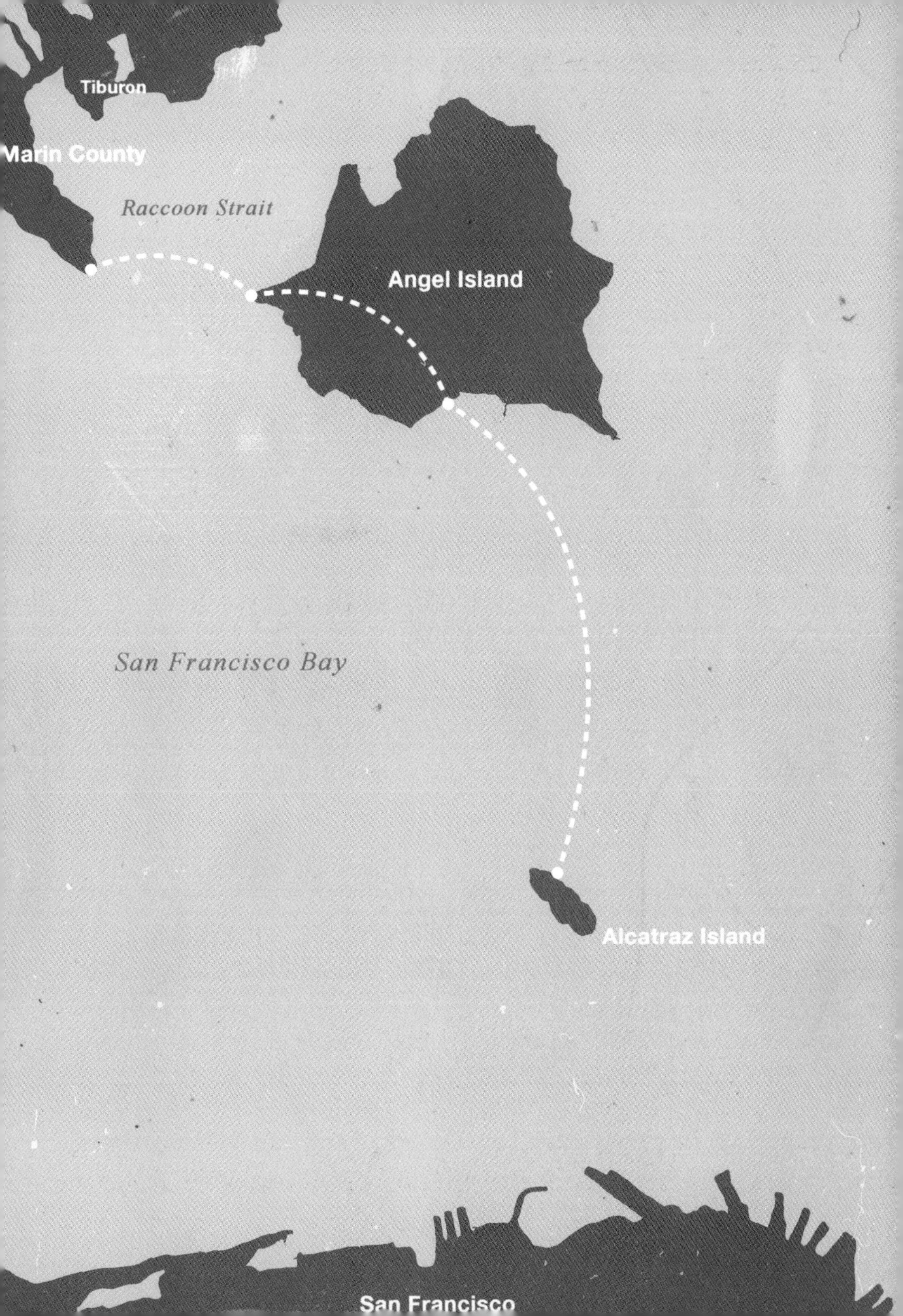
Tiburon
Marin County
Raccoon Strait
Angel Island
San Francisco Bay
Alcatraz Island
San Francisco

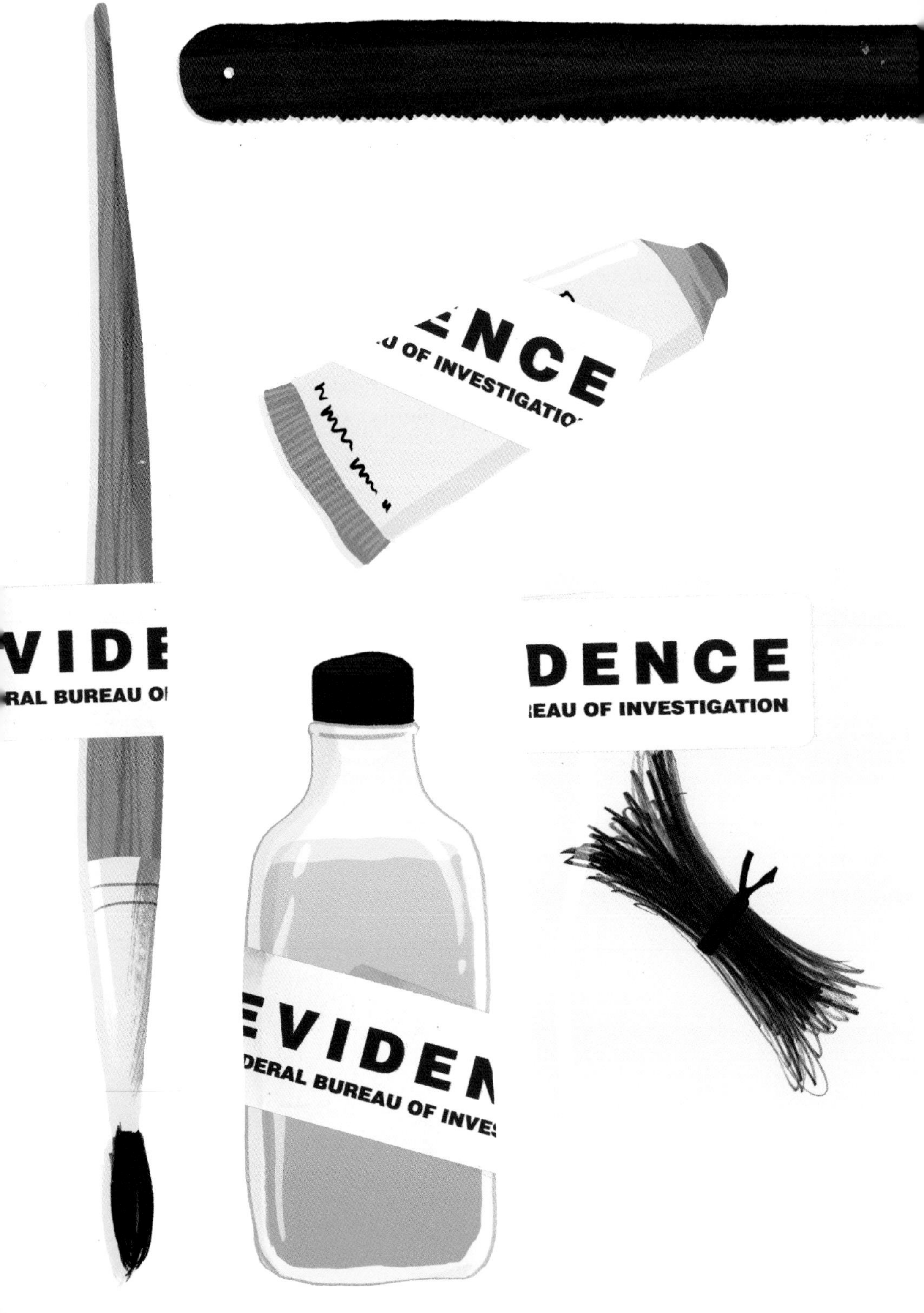

ENCE
AU OF INVESTIGATIO
VIDE
RAL BUREAU OF
DENCE
EAU OF INVESTIGATION
EVIDEN
DERAL BUREAU OF INVES

Aside from locating a road atlas that had a few pages torn out of it in ALLEN WEST'S cell, there were hardly any clues that pointed toward the escapees' intended whereabouts, but investigators were able to recover a plethora of other physical evidence. In JOHN ANGLIN'S cell, the FBI found the *Popular Mechanics* issue detailing the process of vulcanizing rubber. In CLARENCE'S cell they found bundles of human hair, the paint used for the dummy heads, and the green paint used for the false ventilator grills. And in FRANK MORRIS'S cell they found his nail clippers, a few hacksaw blades, and the May 21, 1962, issue of *Sports Illustrated*, which was left open on his table to an ad that depicted a happy couple sitting by a boat—a possible message to the guards.

Eventually, even more clues emerged.

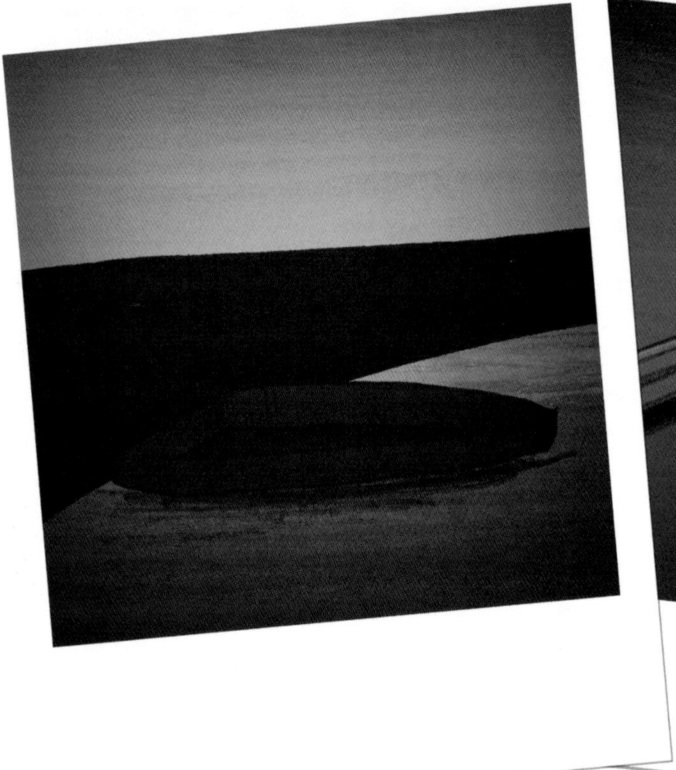
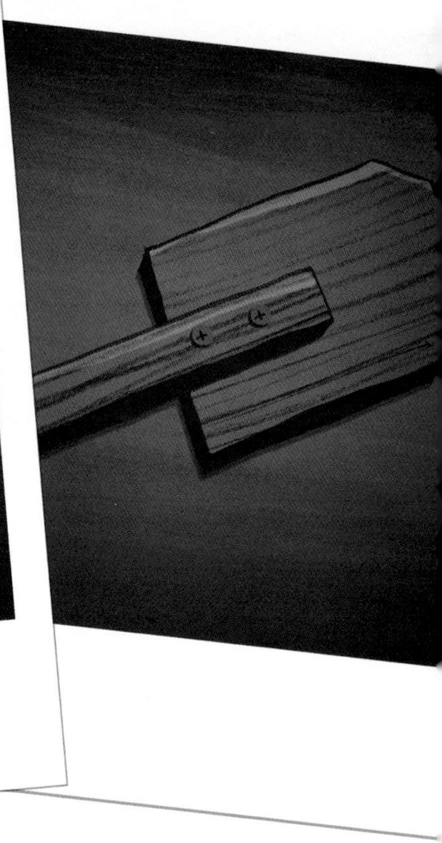

On the morning of the escape, the FBI located a raft on Angel Island. After comparing it to the one left behind in the work area, however, they were able to determine that it was not the raft used in the escape. Later that evening, the Coast Guard found a paddle identical to the one left behind for WEST floating in Raccoon Strait.

On June 15, 1962, a family out for a walk just north of San Francisco found one of the life preservers washed up on FORT CRONKHITE BEACH. Just like another life vest found floating a mere 50 yards from the Alcatraz dock, the air tube had teeth marks all over it—perhaps indicating that the men had struggled to keep it inflated.

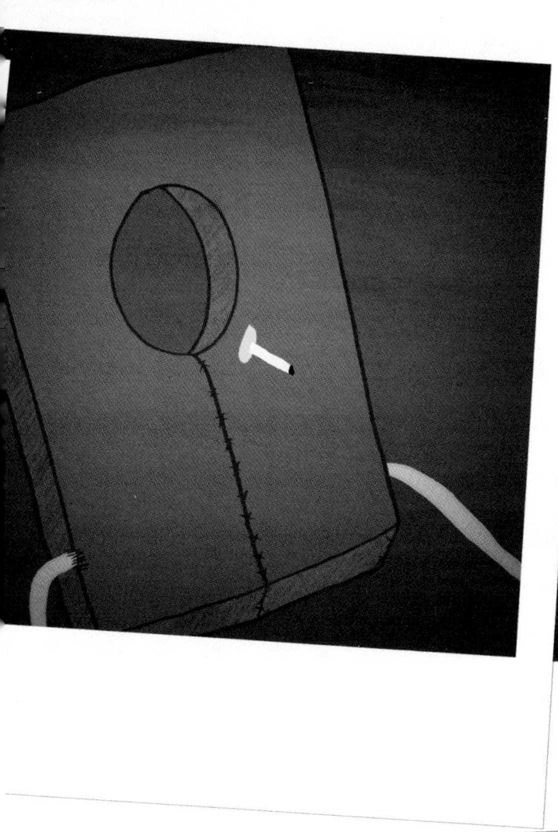

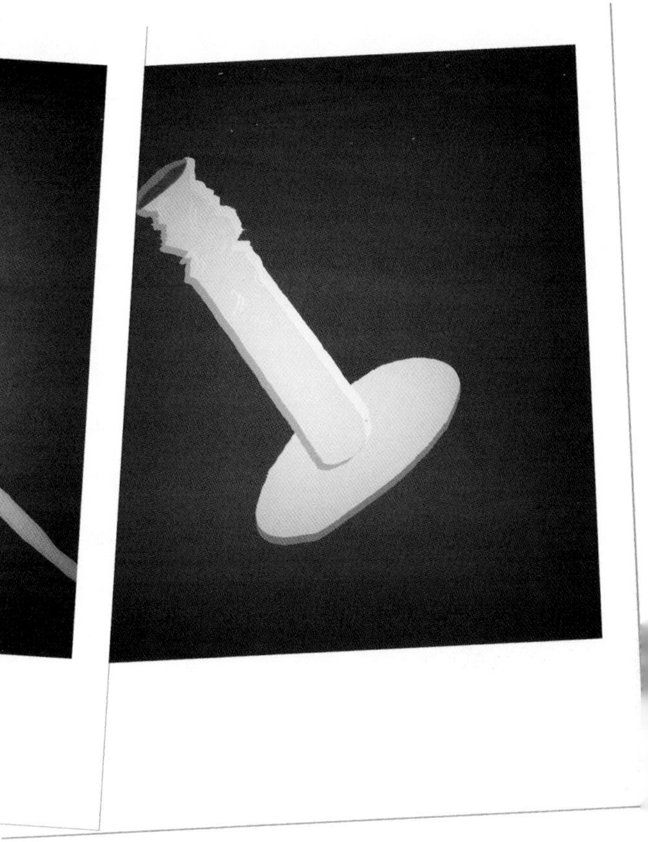

Another piece of evidence recovered from the water was a packet made from raincoat material that contained photographs, letters, addresses, and phone numbers belonging to CLARENCE ANGLIN.

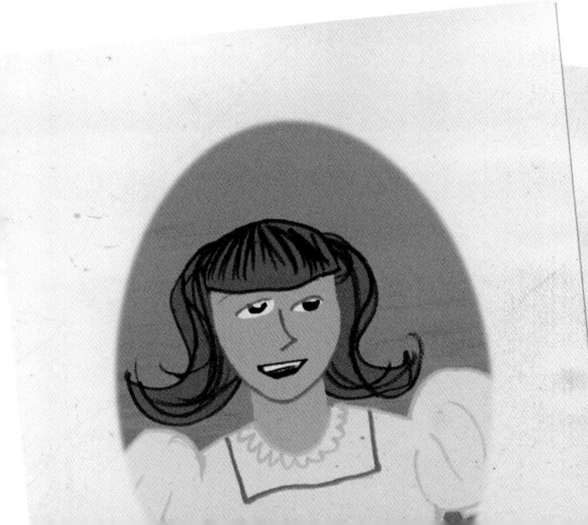

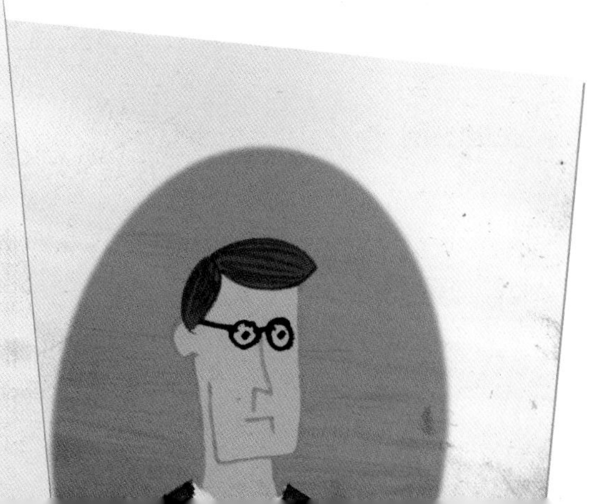

# U.S. 'Devil's Island' Conquered by Girl

'DUMBFOUNDS' FEDERAL OFFICIALS

Reputed unapproachable for a swimmer since it was an early days Spanish fortress ... bay, ... prison ... a rock ... incare ...

## BABE SCOTT HAS FEDERAL MEN AGOG

### Alcatraz Swim Just Ruins Prison Theory

Washington, Oct. 19.—(UP)—Miss Babe Scott of San Francisco can rest assured ...

## GIRL 'ESCAPES' FROM NEW JAIL

... ng out there, because Alcatraz is rocky, isolated dot on the map fro ... which nobody could possibly escal ...

**ANASTASIA 'BABE' SCOTT**
Seventeen-year-old San Francisco girl, who astounded government officials by easily swimming from Alcatraz Island in the Bay just after it had been declared escape from a prison there impossible. Yesterday two other girls made the swim.

## Two More Bay Mermaids Swim To Alcatraz Island, Dumfound Federal Agents

It would have been difficult, though not entirely impossible, to make the swim to shore from Alcatraz, if the life jackets and homemade raft had failed. Back in the 1930s, when it was announced that the prison would be opening, a San Francisco women's group organized an event where high school girls swam out to the island to prove that it was not actually escape-proof.

The attorney general at the time, HOMER S. CUMMINGS, claimed that a prisoner under duress lacked the training and support from boaters that the girls had while making their swim. And Alcatraz was even outfitted with warm showers, so that the inmates would not be able to acclimate themselves to the icy-cold waters of the San Francisco Bay.

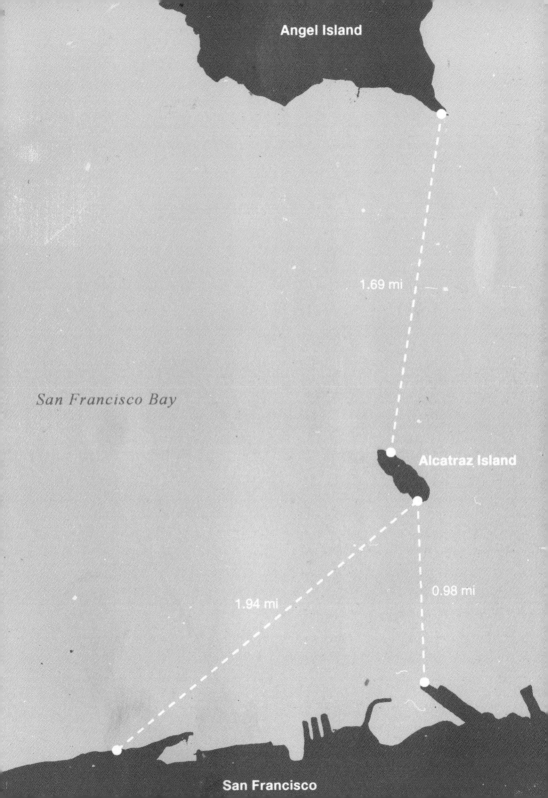

Angel Island

1.69 mi

San Francisco Bay

Alcatraz Island

0.98 mi

1.94 mi

San Francisco

J. STEPHENS

W. GAINEY

In searching the prison, the FBI found several other cells with holes drilled around their air vents, and discovered that at one point prisoners JUNE STEPHENS (AZ-1225), WOODROW WILSON GAINEY (AZ-1520), and ROBBIE WILLIAMS (AZ-1184) had been in on the escape, but they had either quit partway through or been asked to drop out. At any other prison in the world, the other convicts would have snitched on MORRIS, WEST, and the ANGLINS in exchange for a reward. But on Alcatraz there was a real sense of camaraderie among the prisoners.

JAMES "WHITEY" BULGER (AZ-1428), the notorious Boston crime boss turned FBI informant, recalled, "The morning of the escape was one of the happiest moments of my life. . . . The cheers were so loud that it could be heard for miles. . . . It was a moment of freedom for all of us."

R. WILLIAMS

J. BULGER

The day after the escape, a man called the law offices of LESLIE and EUGENIA MACGOWAN, and demanded to speak with LESLIE, who had represented men on Alcatraz in the past. Since he was in court at the time, the receptionist put the man through to LESLIE'S wife, EUGENIA. The caller claimed to be JOHN ANGLIN and wanted to have a meeting set up with the US Marshals' office. When EUGENIA asked what the meeting was about, the man became curt and told her not to ask questions.

EUGENIA prodded for more information, then the man asked, "Do you know who I am?"

At her negative reply, the man simply said, "Read the newspaper," and hung up.

The FBI set up a wiretap on the MACGOWANS' telephone, but the mysterious man never called back.

A couple of weeks later, on June 18, 1962, Warden BLACKWELL received a postcard purportedly from the escapees.

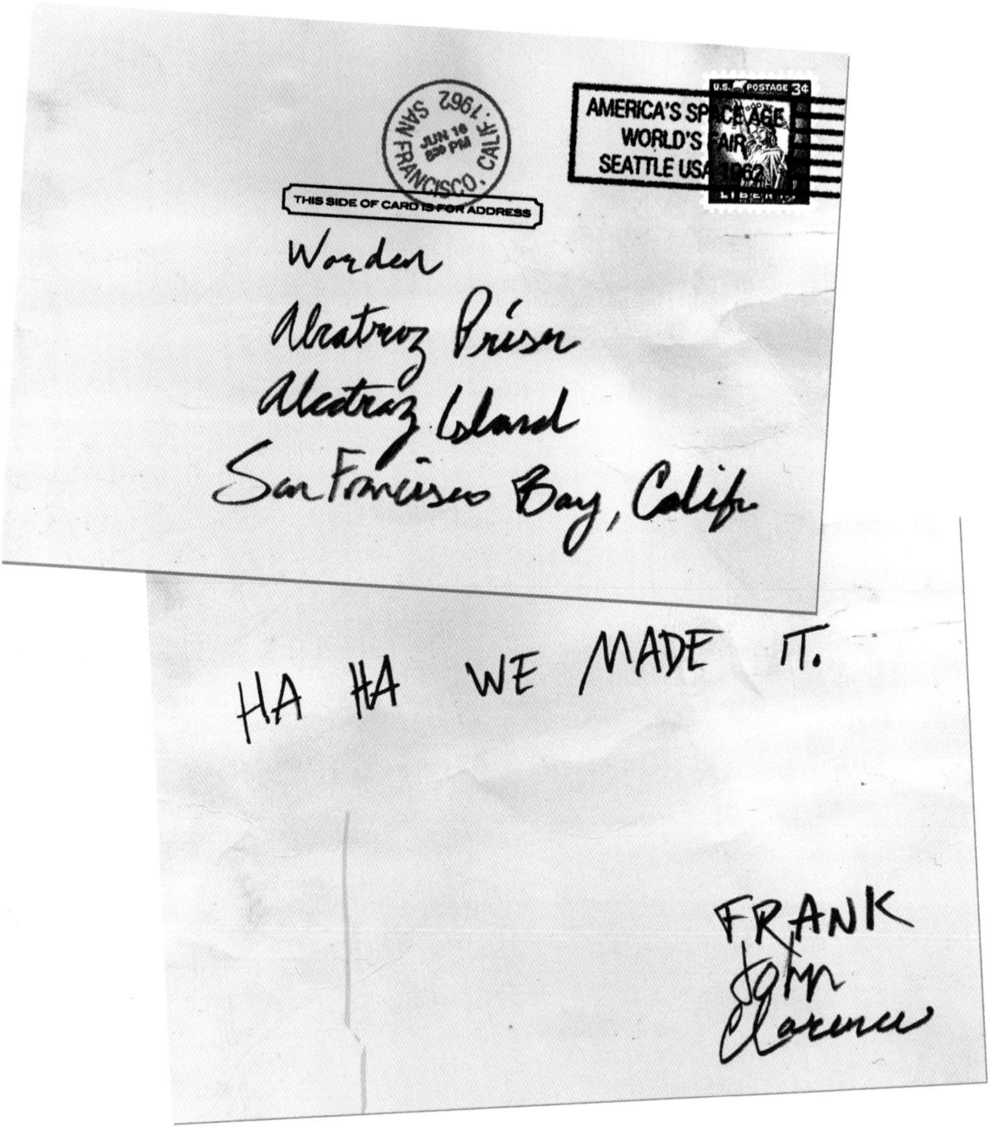
SAN FRANCISCO, CALIF. 1962
JUN 18
AMERICA'S SPACE AGE
WORLD'S FAIR
SEATTLE USA 1962
U.S. POSTAGE 3¢
THIS SIDE OF CARD IS FOR ADDRESS
Warden
Alcatraz Prison
Alcatraz Island
San Francisco Bay, Calif.
HA HA WE MADE IT.
FRANK
John
Clarence

But the FBI's graphologist was able to confirm that the handwriting did not match samples that they had on hand for all three of the men, and that it was most likely a hoax.

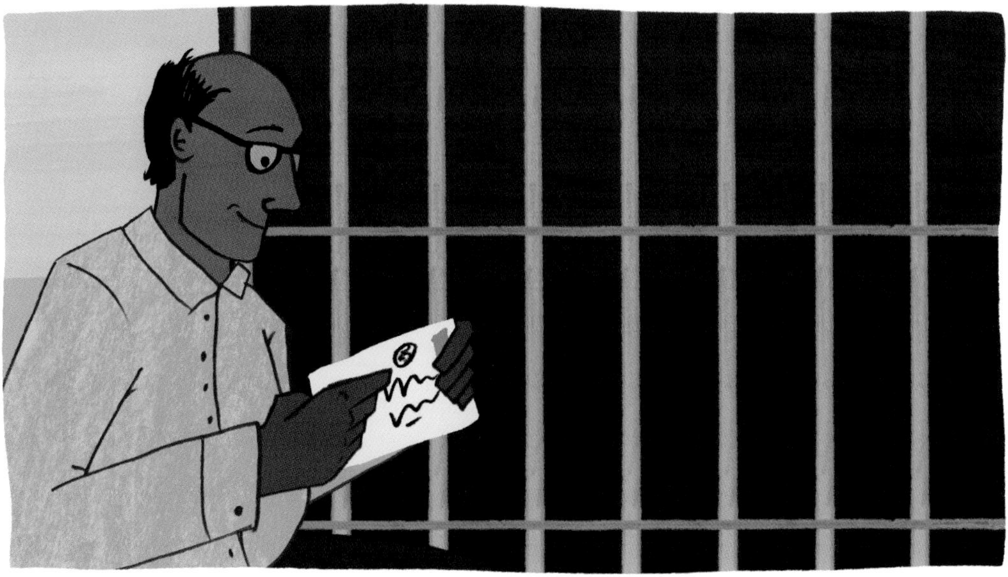

CLARENCE CARNES (AZ-714), on the other hand, a prisoner serving a life sentence, claimed in an interview years after the fact that he had received a postcard shortly after the escape with the code words "Gone fishing" written on it.

To him, anyway, that was proof positive that the trio had indeed made it out alive.

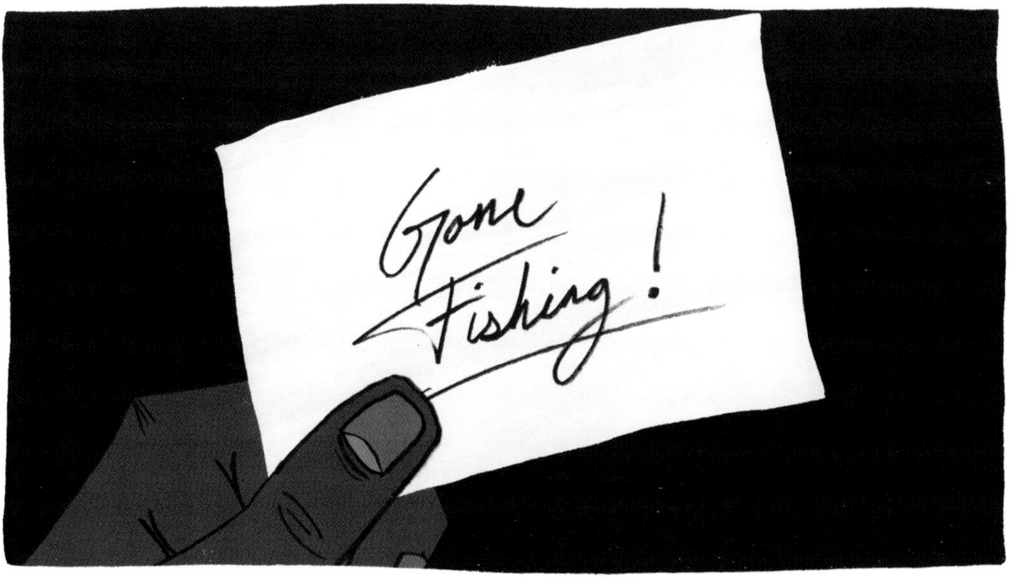
Gone Fishing!

[redacted] while in State Prison he met a prisoner, a white male, early 30's, long black hair, 5' 7", 140 lbs., who knew that he would go back to Lewisburg for violation of parole. The prisoner wanted [redacted] to deliver a message to ANGLIN to the effect that when ANGLIN got out, there would be a boat waiting for him in Florida. [redacted] was transferred back to Lewisburg in December of 1961 and after learning that ANGLIN was gone, told his story to [redacted] at Lewisburg.

[redacted] said that on 10/14/63 he took [redacted] with him to the Hanover Bar on Nine Mile Road in Highland Springs, Va., to get bread and Pepsi Cola. He parked his car in front and entered the tavern about 8:45 P.M., leaving [redacted] in the car. He had been in the bar about 10 minutes and was waiting for his purchases when JOHN ANGLIN came up to him, grabbed his arm and said "Hello [redacted] stated that he was shocked and only said "John, is it you". ANGLIN said "I'll be in touch" and then left the bar with another man. [redacted] described ANGLIN as being identical to the photographs of him. He was wearing a short tan jacket. [redacted] was neatly shaven and had his hair cut short. emphatically insists he saw ANGLIN whom he claims to know very well and that ...

following on ...

...ated June 6, 1963

SA [redacted] ..., 1963, that on ... :00 p.m. he was ... of the O'Hare Ai... ...cott Cafeteria.

... to finish an i... ...scription to CLA... ...rdered a corned ... blue striped was... ...ke to the waitre... ...ng "surly."

[redacted] st... ...his instance unt... a wanted flyer ... June 5, 1963, ... ...ndividual he sa...

...d he, ... ...ich... any ...

OPTIONAL FORM NO. 10
MAY 1962 EDITION
GSA GEN. REG. NO. 27

5010-106

UNITED STATES GOVERNMENT

# Memorandum

TO : DIRECTOR, FBI (76-26295)

DATE: 10/9/63

FROM : SAC, WFO (76-2938) (RUC)

SUBJECT: FRANK LEE MORRIS, aka, WF#307 - FUGITIVE;
JOHN WILLIAM ANGLIN, WF#306 - FUGITIVE;
CLARENCE ANGLIN, WF#305 - FUGITIVE;
[redacted]
EFP; CONSPIRACY
(OO:SF)

Re Bureau telephone call 10/5/63.

Retelcall advised receipt of a telephone call from a man who refused to identify himself. This person said he was acquainted with the Anglin brothers, having attended school with them, and that they were presently in Washington, D.C. He stated he was at the Sheraton-Park Hotel, was in fear of losing his life, and desired to speak with FBI Agents at the intersection in front of the hotel. He said he would be wearing black pants, white shirt and a blue coat, but refused to give his name or further descriptive data saying he could recognize agents.

SAs [redacted] and [redacted] immediately dispatched to scene. They were not approached by anyone nor was anyone observed fitting above description. No further action being taken by WFO.

(2)- Bureau
1- San Francisco (76-2887) (Info)
1- WFO
[redacted]
(4)

76-26295-187

... 11

rmed police
took place
ANGLIN was

...y that the escapees in this matter have ...and co
Further, both advised that ...
...of this escape or the escapees.

...llowing investigation was conducted by

At Dodge City, Kansas:

ked

ng of
snack
icago,

whom he
LIN, sat
utch.
ar summer
e,

individual he believes identical with JOHN WILLIAM ANGLIN. He stated that an sat next to him at the bar of this tavern. He stated ... an individual he believes identical with FRANK LEE MORRIS. was standing with a white man whose... described to be age 22, 6'2", 220 pounds, cocky disposition, who wore a white western hat, dark trousers, and a light shirt.

did not pay
ving
attle Creek
n determined
are Airport

'hare on Ur
.m. and di
nce observi

he believes is JOHN WILLIAM ANGLIN. He conversed with the person told him he was from Los Angeles, California, and was a painter by trade. ...tated he asked this indi- vidual how he liked Minnesota Brand paints, at which point this individual stated that he knew nothing about that brand of paint. ...thought this unusual as Minnesota brand paints are quite prominent. ... stated that he left this tavern after having one bottle of beer about 8:15 P.M., and observed the individual, he believes is FRANK LEE MORRIS, with another man, whom he described to be a white male, age 35-40, dark hair. He stated these individuals were driving a 1950 or 1951 dark blue or possibly green Chevrolet, and that these individuals drove on to U.S. Highway 54, from a side street, located

7

780

87
b7C

wo patro
rge." Subject o

The following information was received from the Butte
FBI, on January 11, 1963:
b7C,b7D

vised
calle
ainte
ANGLI
wher
recall the exact dates ...largest in Montreal. ...ANGLIN.
l, but he did recall he used his true name in
ng.

he dr... blue Mercu... There were two
1961 dark blue Mercu... ANGLIN turned
license plates.
is car. He stated ... the left side
had a band-aid on ...to his apartm
...turned

Tips poured into the FBI from all around the country, but every
one of them turned out to be unfounded.

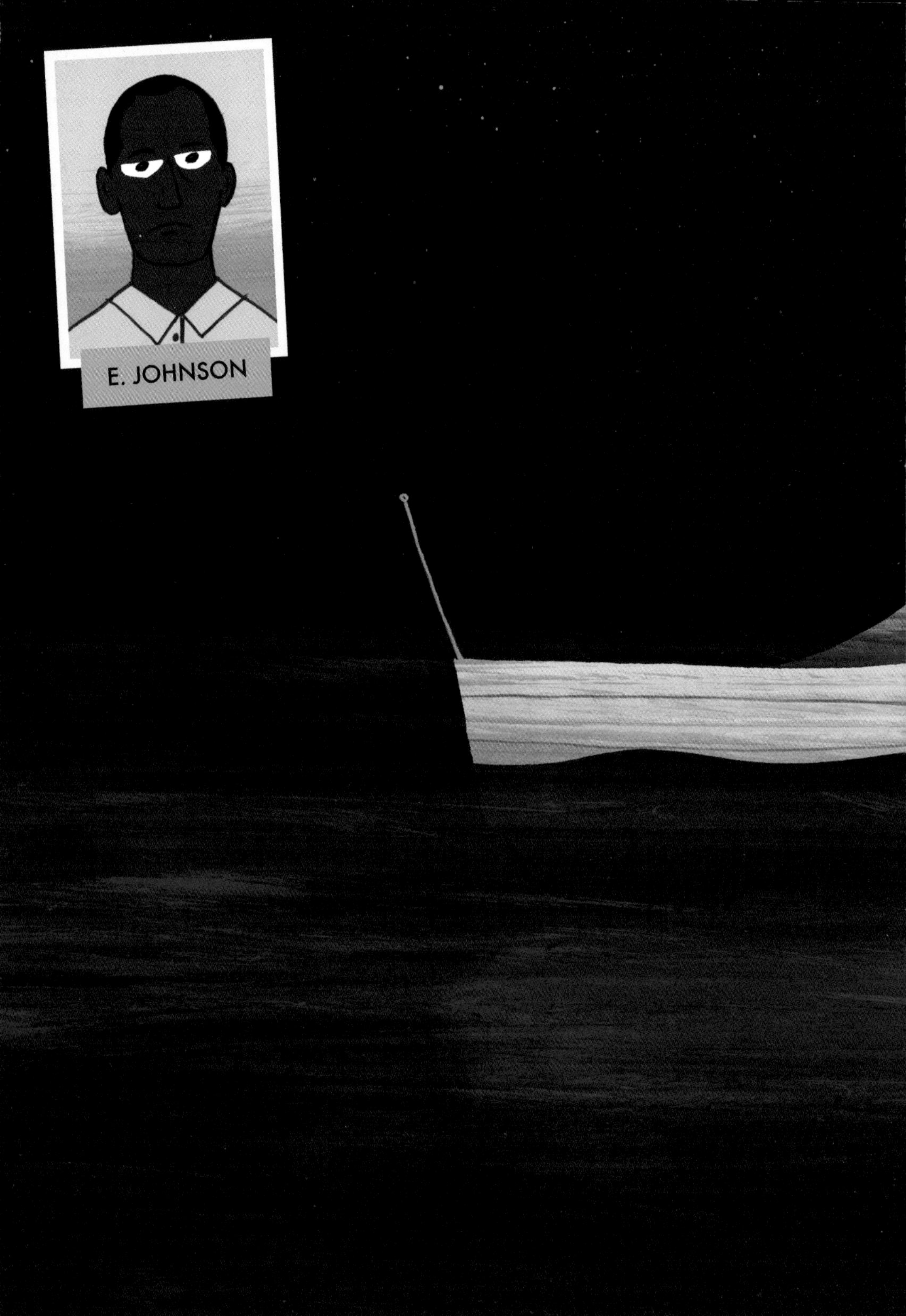
E. JOHNSON

There are several theories regarding the fates of FRANK MORRIS and the ANGLIN brothers. Some have hypothesized that instead of paddling out into the bay, the men made their way around the perimeter of Alcatraz and got a tow from the prison's ferry. The theory goes on to suggest that the "Godfather of Harlem," ELLSWORTH "BUMPY" JOHNSON (AZ-1117), helped secure a boat that picked up the men in the middle of the bay, since he was considered to be one of the only men on Alcatraz with enough pull to arrange something like this.

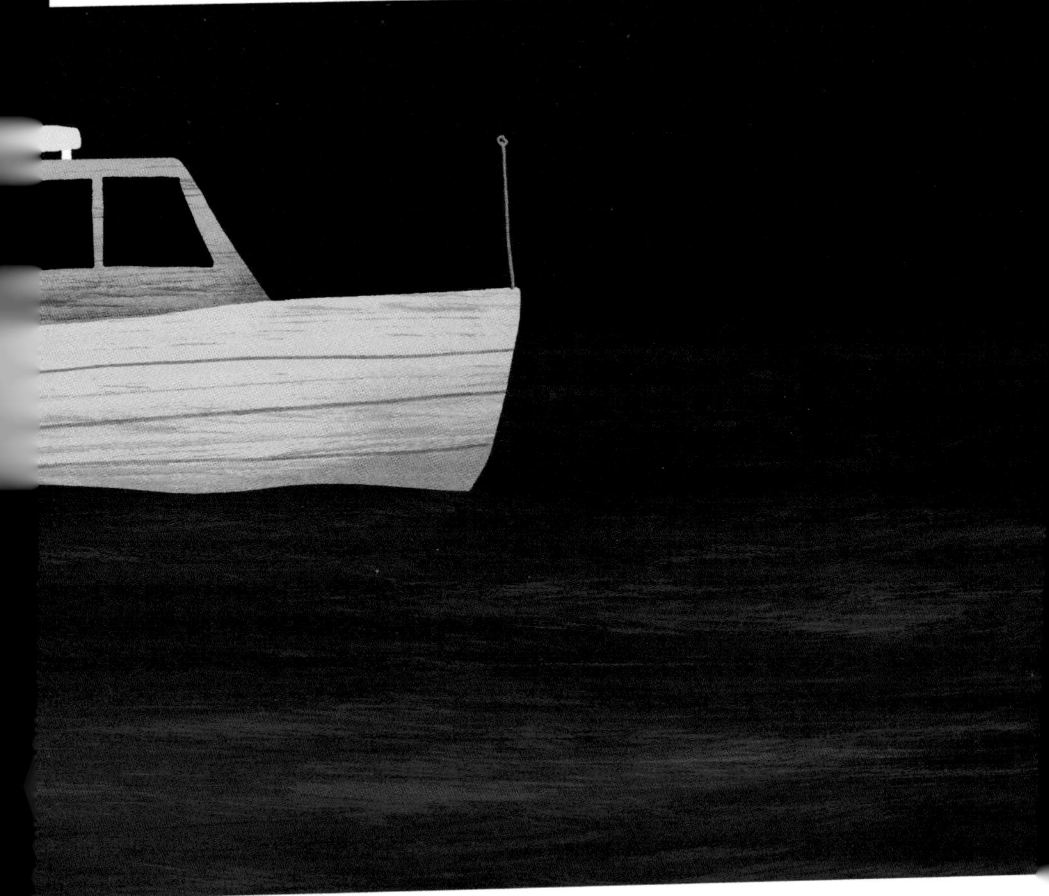

In line with the theory, off-duty police officer ROBERT CHECCH[I] reported seeing a suspicious 30-foot vessel idling in the water betwee[n] Alcatraz and the mainland. The white boat flashed its floodlight and headed out toward open water before disappearing from view.

Even after all this time, the ANGLIN family still holds out hope that their brothers safely made it to shore, and maybe even all the way to BRAZIL.

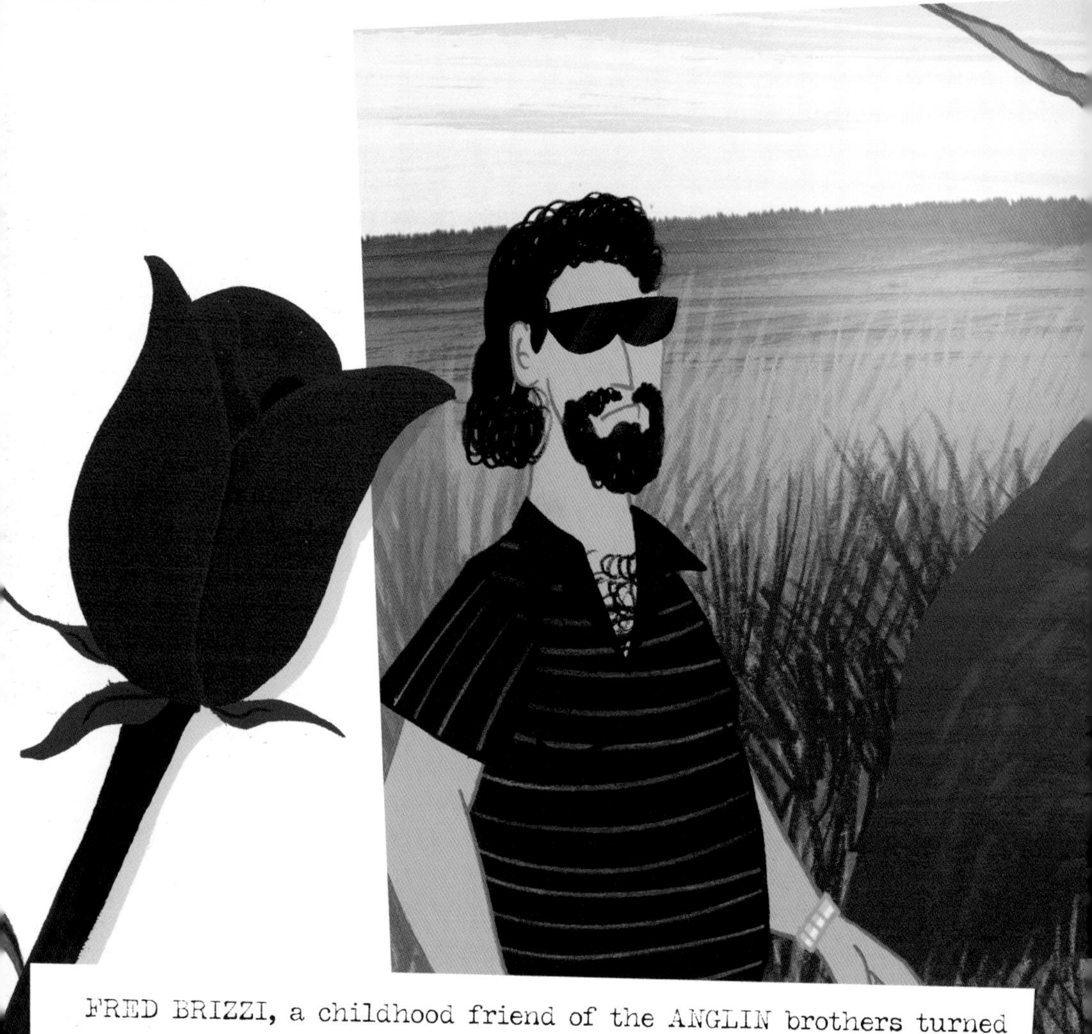

FRED BRIZZI, a childhood friend of the ANGLIN brothers turned drug smuggler, visited the ANGLIN family in 1992. He claimed that back in 1975 during a drug run to Brazil he'd walked into a bar outside RIO DE JANEIRO and bumped into JOHN and CLARENCE. He told the ANGLIN family that the brothers were living modest lives as farmers in the Brazilian countryside, and he even took a photograph of the brothers standing by a termite mound on their property.

A forensic analyst working with the US Marshals' office for a 2015 History Channel documentary compared the Brazilian photograph with other pictures of the brothers and, after examining bone structure, was able to determine that a match—while not 100 percent—was highly likely.

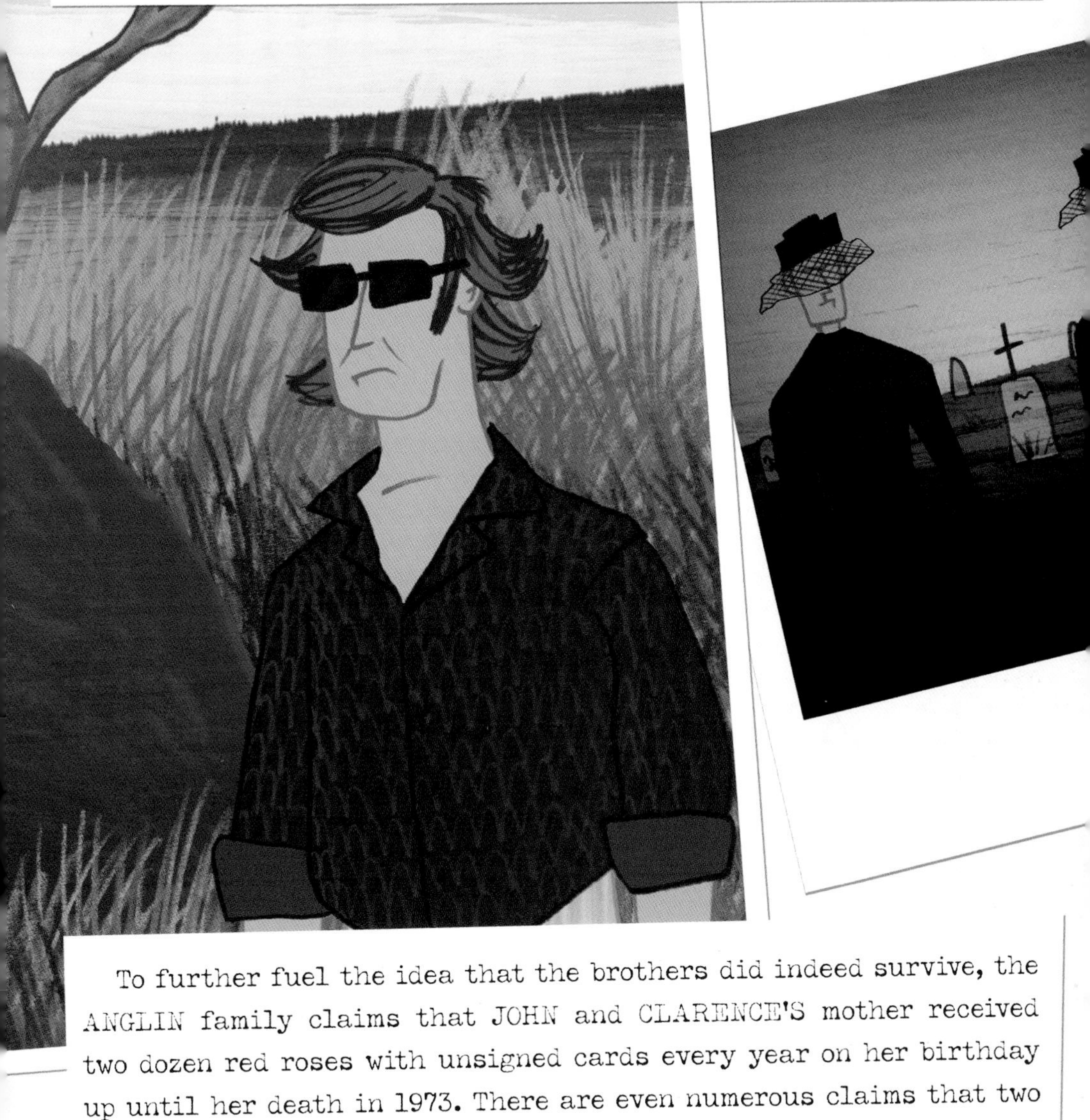

To further fuel the idea that the brothers did indeed survive, the ANGLIN family claims that JOHN and CLARENCE'S mother received two dozen red roses with unsigned cards every year on her birthday up until her death in 1973. There are even numerous claims that two men, disguised as older women, attended the mother's funeral but disappeared before the service was over.

On December 16, 1962, the fourteenth and final escape attempt from Alcatraz took place. Bank robbers JOHN PAUL SCOTT (AZ-1403) and DARL DEE PARKER (AZ-1413) were working their details as part of the kitchen crew. After the corrections officer on duty made his count, the men slipped away and made the final cuts on the bars covering a window that they had presumably been working on for months. From there, the men made their way down to the water.

PARKER was found shortly thereafter clinging to a rock 100 yards offshore. A battered and bruised SCOTT, completely naked except for his socks and suffering from extreme hypothermia, was discovered by two teenagers at FORT POINT—just over three miles away from The Rock at the base of the GOLDEN GATE BRIDGE, thus proving that it was absolutely possible for an inmate to survive the treacherous swim to the mainland.

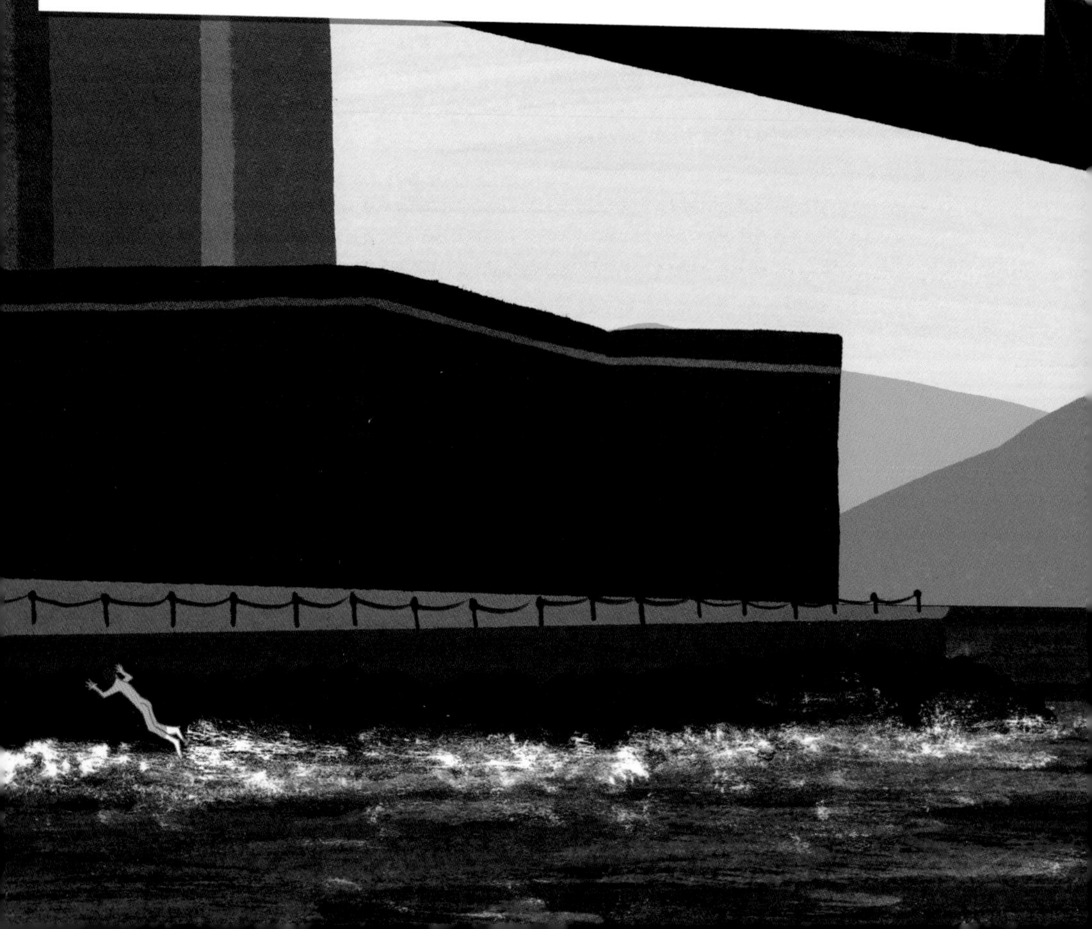

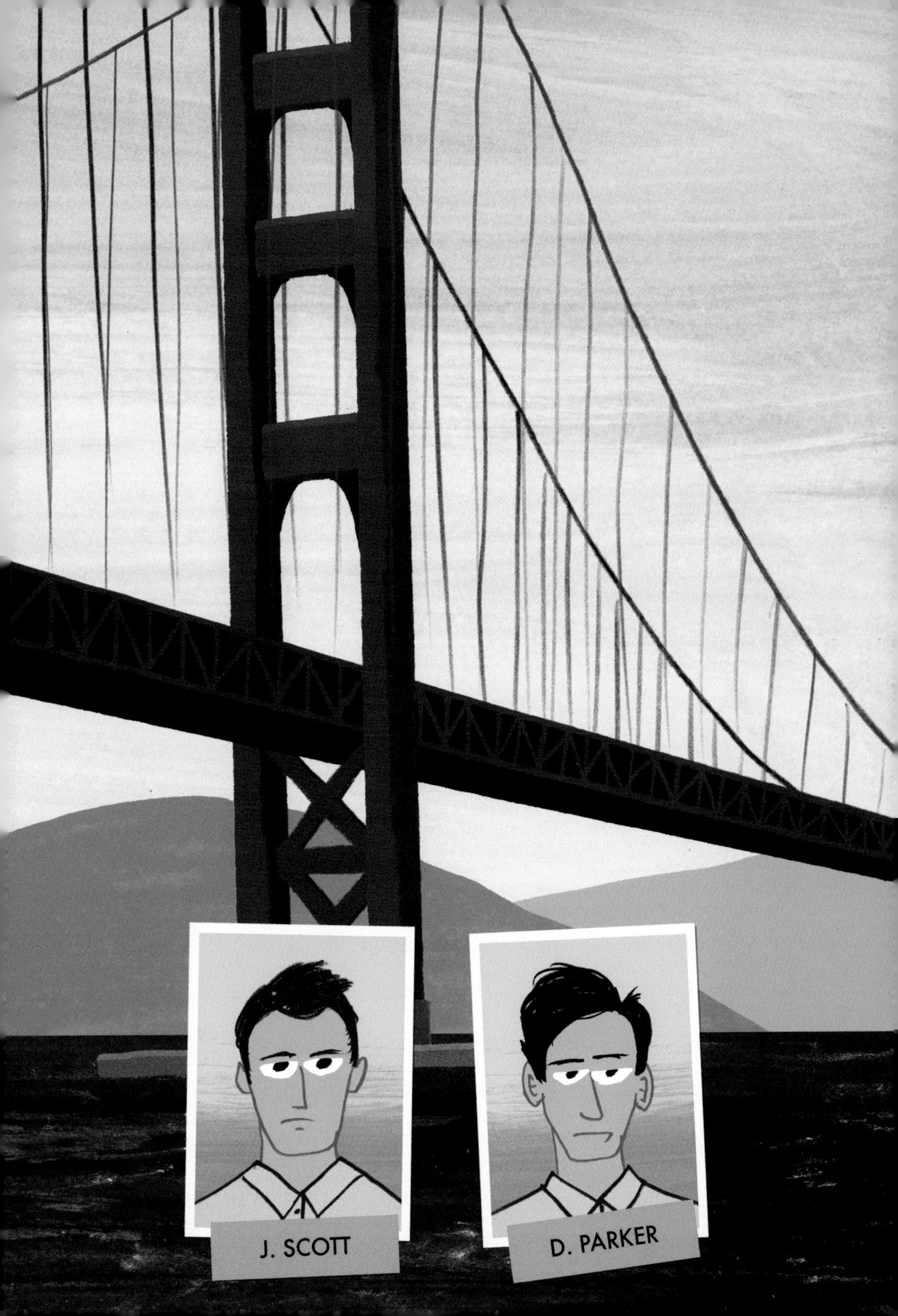
J. SCOTT
D. PARKER

It is not known whether FRANK MORRIS and JOHN and CLARENCE ANGLIN survived that evening. But it is the official opinion of the FBI—despite a complete lack of hard evidence—that the three escaped convicts most likely drowned in the San Francisco Bay on that fateful evening in 1962.

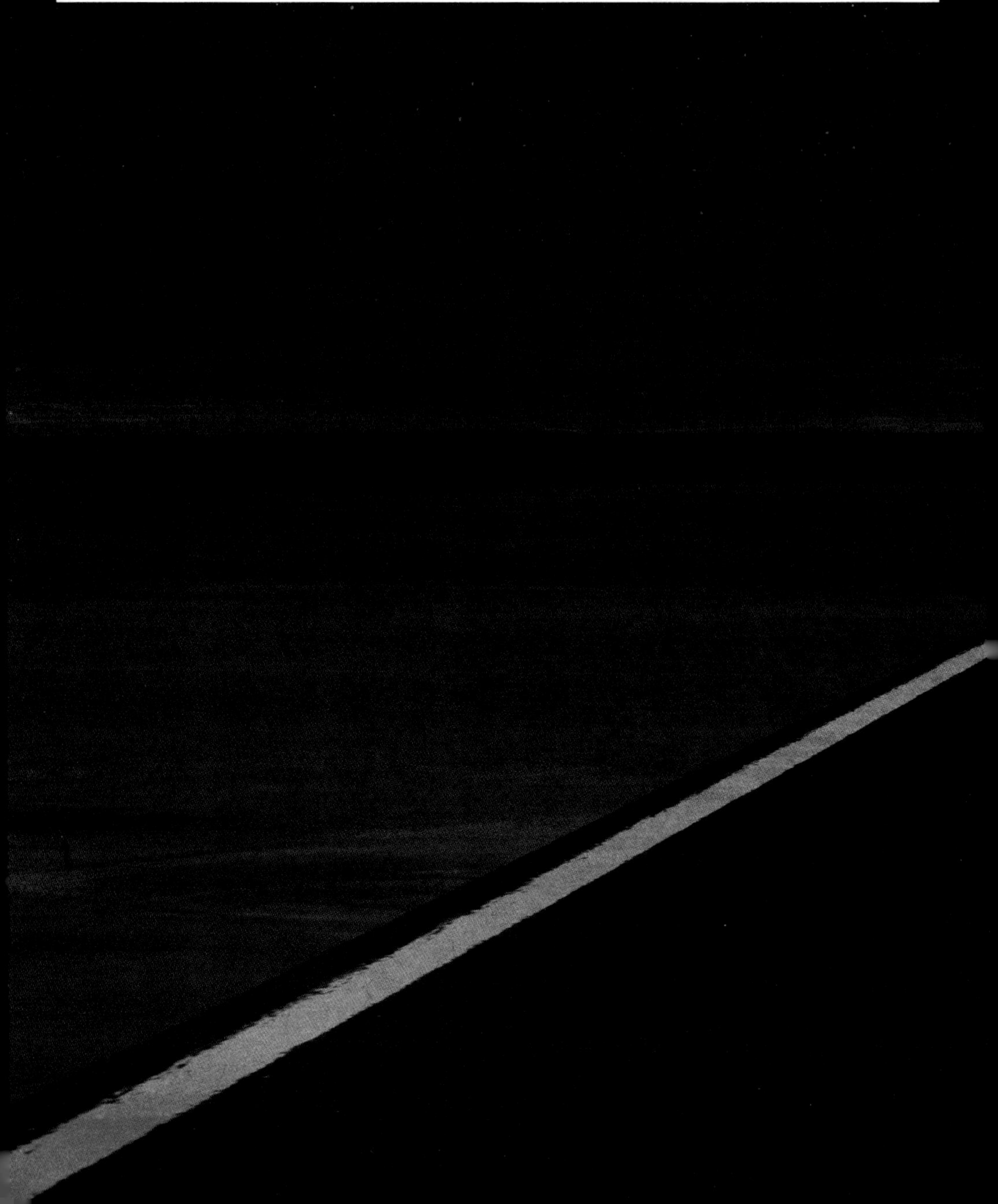

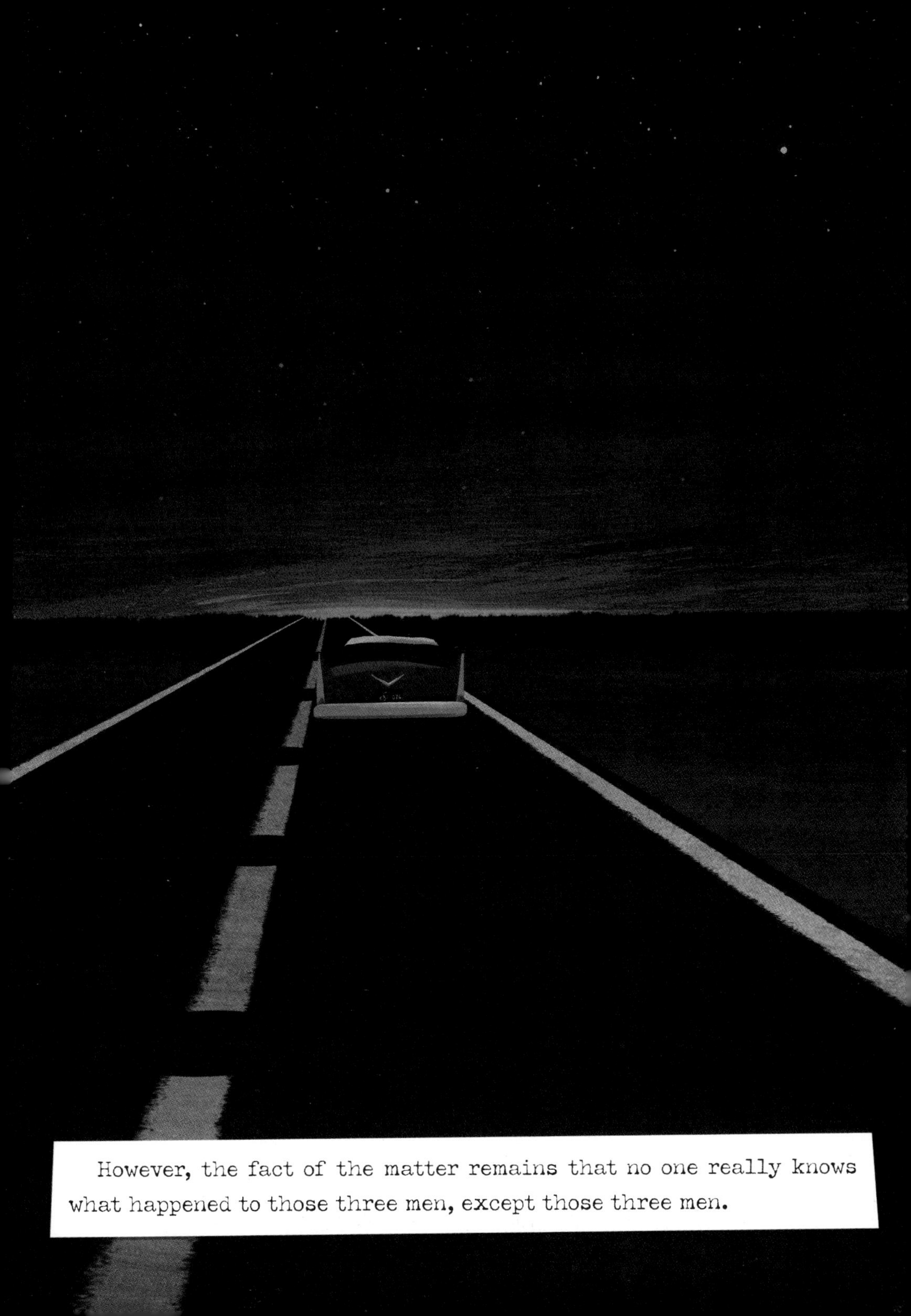
However, the fact of the matter remains that no one really knows what happened to those three men, except those three men.

In its heyday, Alcatraz was home to a rogues' gallery of criminals that reads like a who's who of the FBI's most-wanted list, and in its first year alone housed the headline-grabbing gangsters ALPHONSE "SCARFACE" CAPONE (AZ-85) and GEORGE "MACHINE GUN" KELLY BARNES (AZ-117). But after twenty-nine years, the daily operational costs had ballooned to more than triple those of other federal prisons. That, coupled with the fact that the price to repair the eroded concrete structure after a century of saltwater damage exceeded millions of dollars, led Attorney General ROBERT F. KENNEDY to make the decision to shutter the doors of Alcatraz for good.

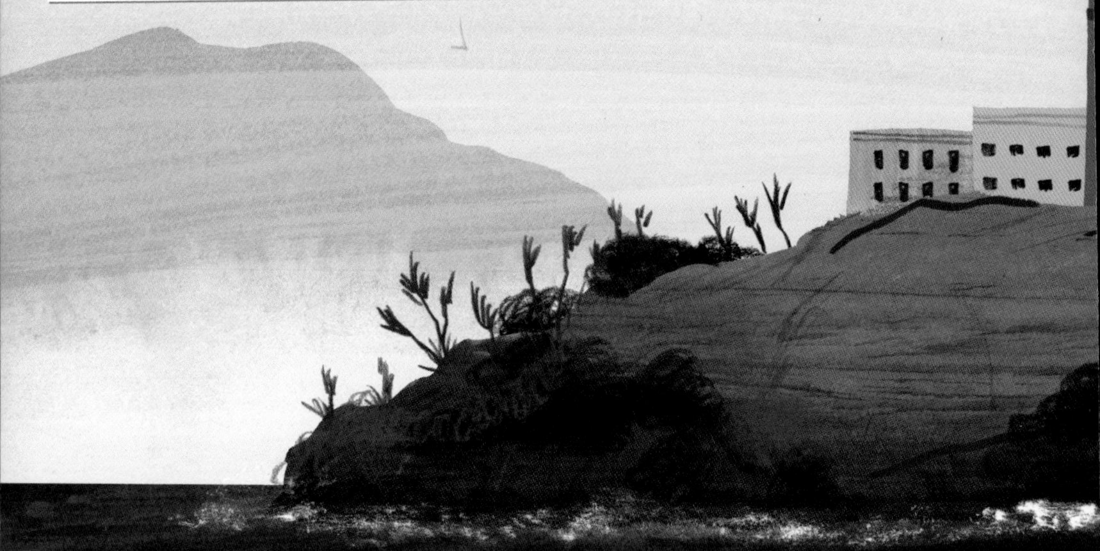

On March 21, 1963—less than a year after FRANK MORRIS and the ANGLIN brothers had made their great escape—the last prisoners were shipped off the island and transferred to other federal prisons.

Smuggler FRANK C. WEATHERMAN (AZ-1576) was the last inmate to board the boat off the island, and when asked by the press for his thoughts on the closing of the prison, he replied, "Alcatraz was never good for anybody."

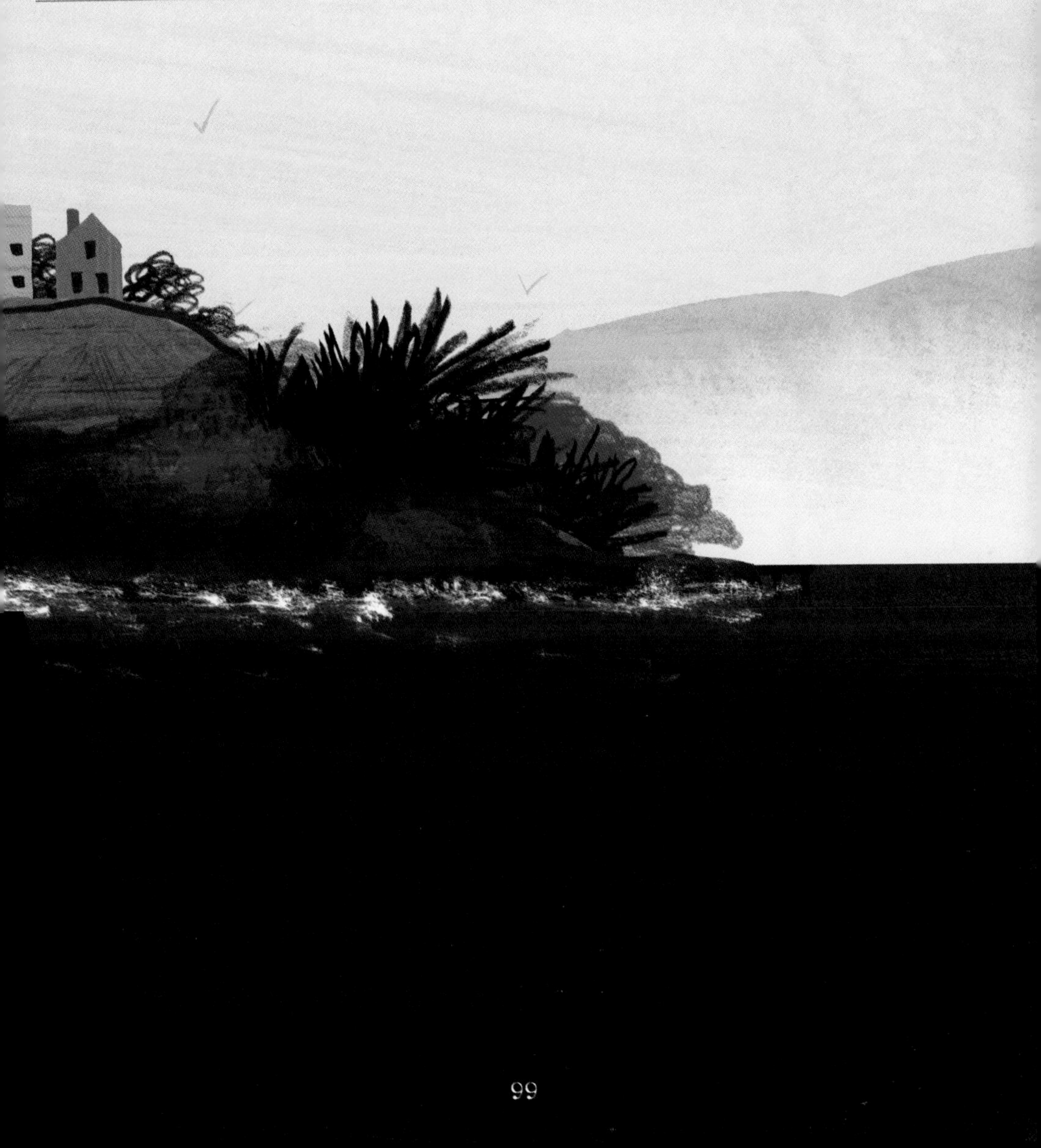

# PHOTOS FROM THE FILES

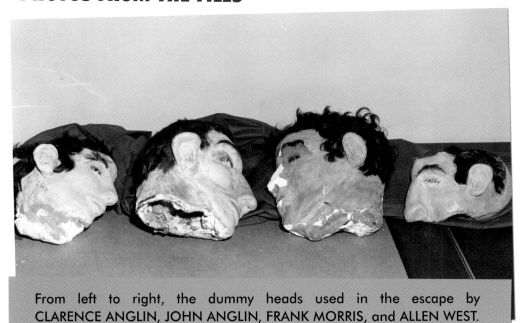

From left to right, the dummy heads used in the escape by CLARENCE ANGLIN, JOHN ANGLIN, FRANK MORRIS, and ALLEN WEST.

The dummy in CLARENCE ANGLIN'S bed illustrating how it was positioned to fool the guards.

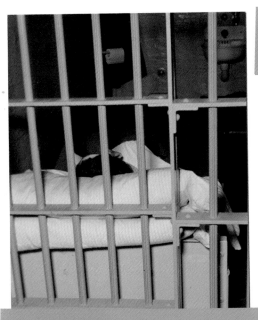

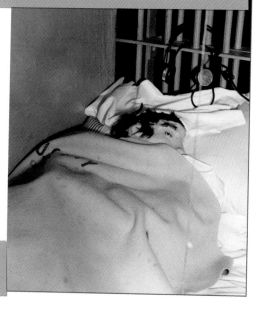

A view of the dummy head in FRANK MORRIS'S cell.

A guard examines the ventilation hole in FRANK MORRIS'S cell.

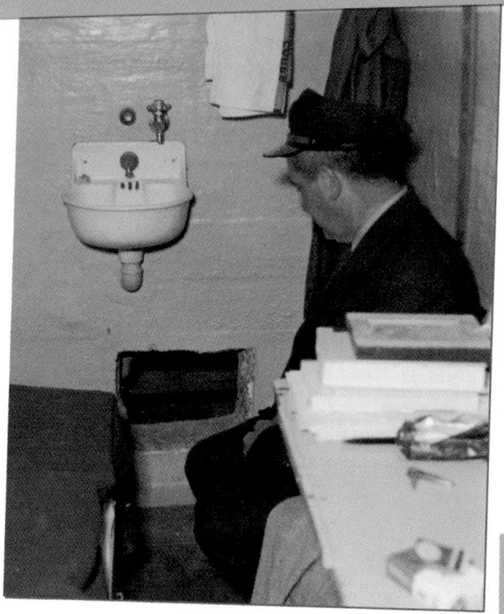

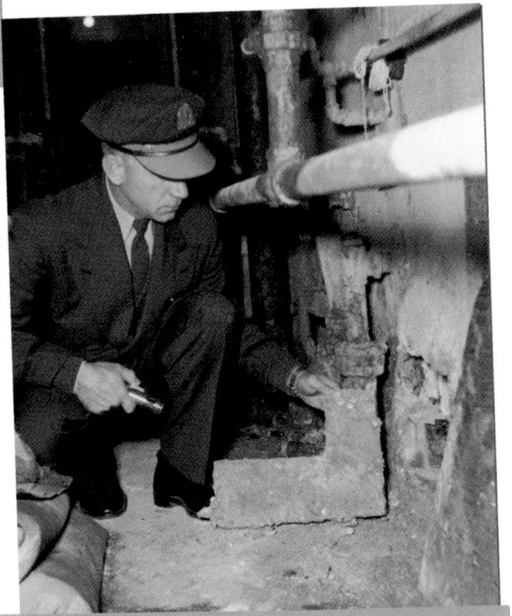

A view of the escape hole from the utility corridor.

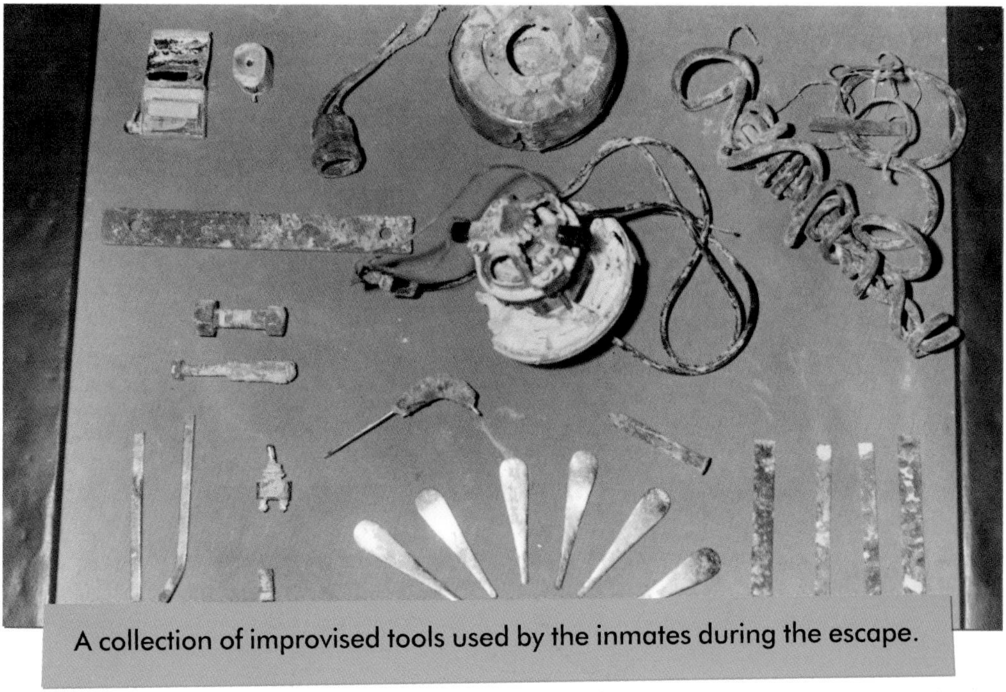

A collection of improvised tools used by the inmates during the escape.

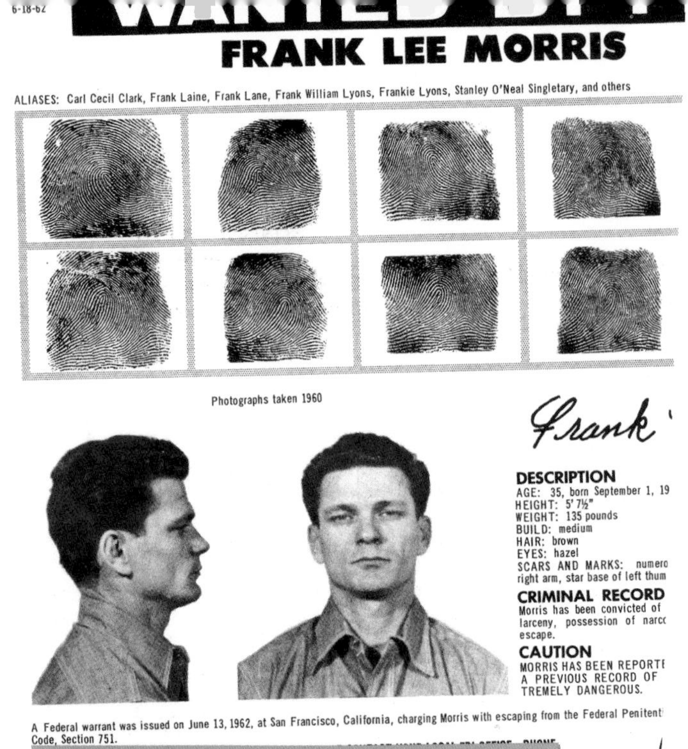
6-18-62

WANTED BY

FRANK LEE MORRIS

ALIASES: Carl Cecil Clark, Frank Laine, Frank Lane, Frank William Lyons, Frankie Lyons, Stanley O'Neal Singletary, and others

Photographs taken 1960

Frank

DESCRIPTION
AGE: 35, born September 1, 19
HEIGHT: 5' 7½"
WEIGHT: 135 pounds
BUILD: medium
HAIR: brown
EYES: hazel
SCARS AND MARKS: numero
right arm, star base of left thum

CRIMINAL RECORD
Morris has been convicted of
larceny, possession of narc
escape.

CAUTION
MORRIS HAS BEEN REPORTE
A PREVIOUS RECORD OF
TREMELY DANGEROUS.

A Federal warrant was issued on June 13, 1962, at San Francisco, California, charging Morris with escaping from the Federal Penitent
Code, Section 751.

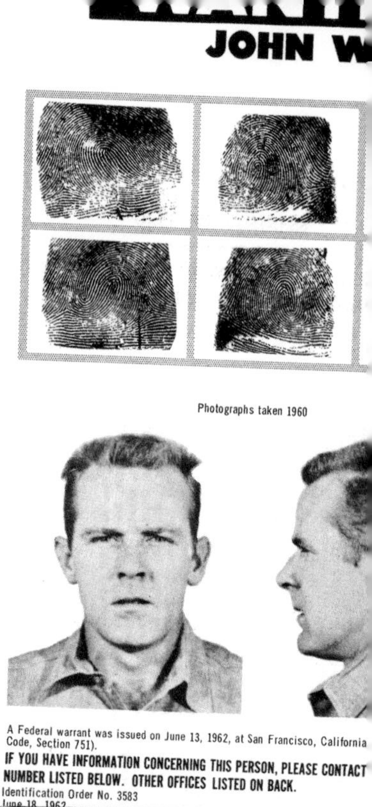
JOHN W

Photographs taken 1960

A Federal warrant was issued on June 13, 1962, at San Francisco, California
Code, Section 751).

IF YOU HAVE INFORMATION CONCERNING THIS PERSON, PLEASE CONTACT
NUMBER LISTED BELOW. OTHER OFFICES LISTED ON BACK.
Identification Order No. 3583
June 18, 1962

The workshop used by the inmates in the area on top of the cell blocks.

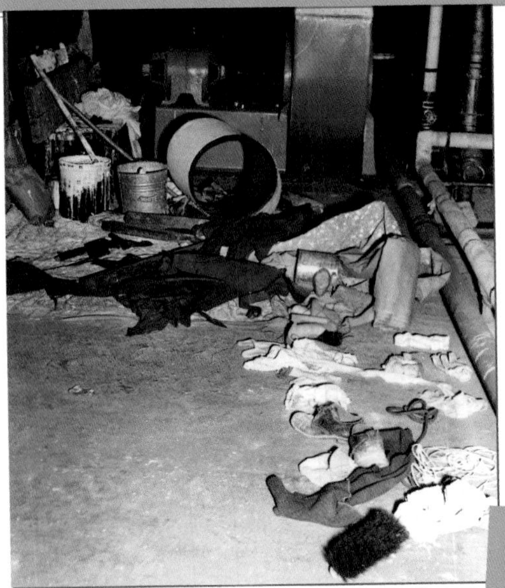

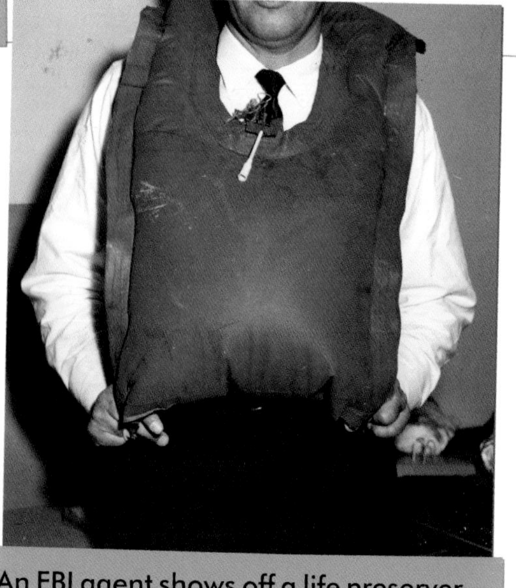

An FBI agent shows off a life preserver made from raincoats.

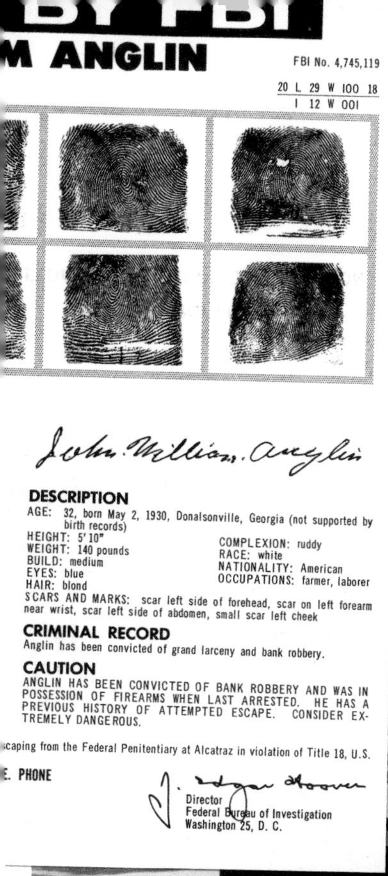

BY FBI

M ANGLIN

FBI No. 4,745,119

20 L 29 W IOO 18
I 12 W OOI

*John William Anglin*

**DESCRIPTION**

AGE: 32, born May 2, 1930, Donalsonville, Georgia (not supported by birth records)
HEIGHT: 5'10"
WEIGHT: 140 pounds
BUILD: medium
EYES: blue
HAIR: blond
COMPLEXION: ruddy
RACE: white
NATIONALITY: American
OCCUPATIONS: farmer, laborer
SCARS AND MARKS: scar left side of forehead, scar on left forearm near wrist, scar left side of abdomen, small scar left cheek

**CRIMINAL RECORD**

Anglin has been convicted of grand larceny and bank robbery.

**CAUTION**

ANGLIN HAS BEEN CONVICTED OF BANK ROBBERY AND WAS IN POSSESSION OF FIREARMS WHEN LAST ARRESTED. HE HAS A PREVIOUS HISTORY OF ATTEMPTED ESCAPE. CONSIDER EXTREMELY DANGEROUS.

scaping from the Federal Penitentiary at Alcatraz in violation of Title 18, U.S.

E. PHONE

*J. Edgar Hoover*
Director
Federal Bureau of Investigation
Washington 25, D. C.

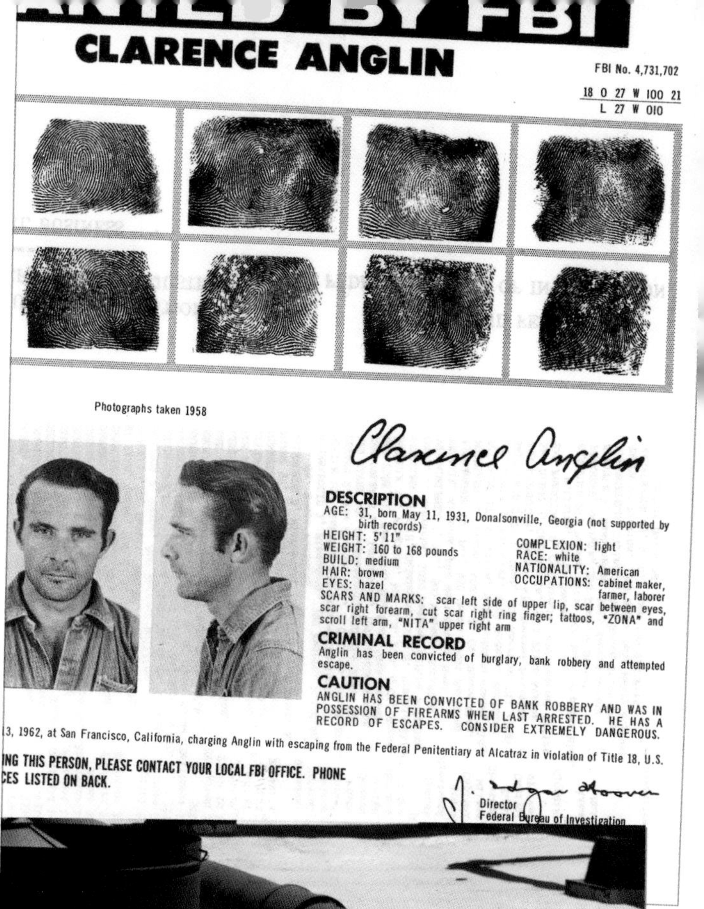

ANTED BY FBI

CLARENCE ANGLIN

FBI No. 4,731,702

18 O 27 W IOO 21
L 27 W OIO

Photographs taken 1958

*Clarence Anglin*

**DESCRIPTION**

AGE: 31, born May 11, 1931, Donalsonville, Georgia (not supported by birth records)
HEIGHT: 5'11"
WEIGHT: 160 to 168 pounds
BUILD: medium
HAIR: brown
EYES: hazel
COMPLEXION: light
RACE: white
NATIONALITY: American
OCCUPATIONS: cabinet maker, farmer, laborer
SCARS AND MARKS: scar left side of upper lip, scar between eyes, scar right forearm, cut scar right ring finger; tattoos, "ZONA" and scroll left arm, "NITA" upper right arm

**CRIMINAL RECORD**

Anglin has been convicted of burglary, bank robbery and attempted escape.

**CAUTION**

ANGLIN HAS BEEN CONVICTED OF BANK ROBBERY AND WAS IN POSSESSION OF FIREARMS WHEN LAST ARRESTED. HE HAS A RECORD OF ESCAPES. CONSIDER EXTREMELY DANGEROUS.

13, 1962, at San Francisco, California, charging Anglin with escaping from the Federal Penitentiary at Alcatraz in violation of Title 18, U.S.

ING THIS PERSON, PLEASE CONTACT YOUR LOCAL FBI OFFICE. PHONE
CES LISTED ON BACK.

*J. Edgar Hoover*
Director
Federal Bureau of Investigation

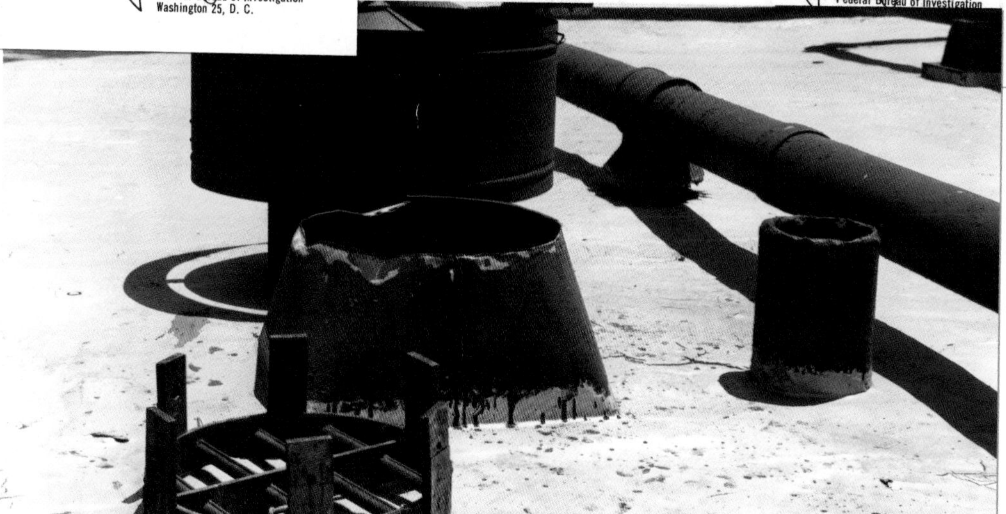

The ventilator hole on the roof of the cell house where the prisoners made their escape.

On October 25, 1973, Alcatraz Island was opened to the public as part of the National Park Service's GOLDEN GATE NATIONAL RECREATION AREA. It is visited by over one million tourists every year.

On December 31, 1979, after exhausting every feasible lead, the FBI officially turned the case of FRANK MORRIS and JOHN and CLARENCE ANGLIN over to the US Marshals' office, which continues to investigate these dangerous fugitives in the unlikely event that the trio are still alive today.

Should you or your family have any knowledge as to the whereabouts of these escaped prisoners, please contact your local US Marshals' office.

## SOURCES

All website URLs are accurate as of date of publication.

OVERVIEW OF THE CASE (INCLUDING FBI PRIMARY SOURCE MATERIALS):

"Alcatraz Escape." Federal Bureau of Investigation, US Department of Justice. www.fbi.gov/history/famous-cases/alcatraz-escape.

Alcatraz History. Ocean View Publishing. www.alcatrazhistory.com.

Bruce, J. Campbell. *Escape from Alcatraz.* New York: McGraw-Hill, 1963.

Esslinger, Michael. *Alcatraz: A History of the Penitentiary Years.* San Francisco: Ocean View Publishing, 2016.

Esslinger, Michael, and David Widner. *Escaping Alcatraz: The Untold Story of the Greatest Prison Break in American History.* San Francisco: Ocean View Publishing, 2017.

THE NATIONAL PARK SERVICE PROVIDED SOME GREAT VISUAL RESOURCES:

"Alcatraz Island: Maps." National Park Service, US Department of the Interior. http://home.nps.gov/alca/planyourvisit/maps.htm.

"Museum Collections at The Rock: Alcatraz Island." National Park Service, US Department of the Interior. www.nps.gov/museum/exhibits/alca/overview.html.

INFORMATION ABOUT PLUMBING:

Butch. "Salt Water Corrosion Effects on Concrete." Pond Armor. January 14, 2008. www.pondarmor.com/salt-water-corrosion-effects-on-concrete/.

Nestor, Bill. "Escape to Alcatraz: A Low-Pressure Wastewater Disposal System Solves the Problem." Pumps & Systems. December 17, 2011. www.pumpsandsystems.com/escape-alcatraz-low-pressure-wastewater-disposal-system-solves-problem.

THE CONVICTS' MAGAZINES:

Brogan, Dan. "Rubber Geese." *Popular Mechanics*, November 1960.

Collins, William with Arthur Zich. "Family Outboarding." *Sports Illustrated*, May 21, 1962.

"Your Life Preserver—How Will It Behave If You Need It?" *Popular Mechanics*, March 1962.

**COMING SOON:**

THE 500 MILLION

CASE No. 003 DOLLAR HEIST